To:

....

From:

....

On this Date:

....

PRAYERS AND PROMISES for Kids

Prayers and Promises for Boys Print ISBN 978-1-63609-515-8
Prayers and Promises for Girls Print ISBN 978-1-63609-516-5

Published by Barbour Publishing, Inc., 1810 Barbour Drive, Uhrichsville, Ohio 44683, www.barbourbooks.com

Our mission is to inspire the world with the life-changing message of the Bible.

Printed in the United States of America.

001563 0323 BP

JoAnne Simmons

PRAYERS AND PROMISES for Kids

200 Days of Inspiration and Encouragement

Through [God's] shining-
greatness and perfect life,
He has given us promises.
These promises are of great
worth and no amount of
money can buy them.

2 Peter 1:4

Jesus says yes to all of God's many promises. It is through Jesus that we say, "Let it be so," when we give thanks to God. God is the One Who makes our faith and your faith strong in Christ. He has set us apart for Himself. He has put His mark on us to show we belong to Him. His Spirit is in our hearts to prove this.

2 Corinthians 1:20–22

You probably make promises sometimes, and hopefully you keep them as best you can! But keeping promises can be hard. Sometimes we forget our promises, and sometimes we break them when we really didn't mean to. The things of this world come and go, and promises do too.

But we can *always* count on the promises of God. They don't come and go. They stand forever. We can trust them because our heavenly Father is so good and faithful. He will never break a promise, and He sent His Son, Jesus, to show they are all true. We find God's promises in His Word, and when we study His Word and respond in prayer—like you can as you read this book—we grow closer to our heavenly Father, who is the very best promise keeper ever!

DAY 1

Full of Joy

Be full of joy always because you belong to the Lord. Again I say, be full of joy! Let all people see how gentle you are. The Lord is coming again soon. Do not worry. Learn to pray about everything. Give thanks to God as you ask Him for what you need. The peace of God is much greater than the human mind can understand. This peace will keep your hearts and minds through Christ Jesus.

PHILIPPIANS 4:4–7

Dear Lord, I get scared and worried sometimes. There's a lot I don't understand about the world. But I understand this scripture that promises that I belong to You, and that's what matters most. I believe You are the almighty Creator God. Nothing and no one is more powerful than You! I believe You sent Your Son, Jesus, to die on the cross for my sin. I admit my sin, and I know that I need Jesus as my Savior. Now Your Holy Spirit is within me, and I am Yours! You will care for me and guide me through everything that comes my way! Amazing! Thank You for filling me with joy and peace as I trust in You and Your great big love. Amen.

DAY 2

Thinking about Good Things

Keep your minds thinking about whatever is true, whatever is respected, whatever is right, whatever is pure, whatever can be loved, and whatever is well thought of. If there is anything good and worth giving thanks for, think about these things. Keep on doing all the things you learned and received and heard from me. Do the things you saw me do. Then the God Who gives peace will be with you.

PHILIPPIANS 4:8–9

Dear Father God, sometimes I'm mean and angry in my mind or think about things I shouldn't. Please forgive me. Please help me to remember this scripture. I want to do a better job obeying it. Help me to learn and remember truth and teaching from Your Word. Help me to focus on good and joyful things that will bring me blessings, and let me share those blessings with others. Amen.

DAY 3

God Cares

Give all your worries to Him
because He cares for you.
1 Peter 5:7

Father God, I'm so relieved Your Word tells me to give all my worries and cares to You! Thank You for wanting to take them away from me. I'm picturing myself taking hold of these fears and anxious thoughts and throwing them toward You as hard as I can. I know You will catch and destroy them. Then You'll give me Your love and peace in place of them. Every single day of my life, help me to keep trusting more and more in Your loving care for me. Amen.

DAY 4

The Helper Is the Holy Spirit

[Jesus said,] "I have told you these things while I am still with you. The Helper is the Holy Spirit. The Father will send Him in My place. He will teach you everything and help you remember everything I have told you. Peace I leave with you. My peace I give to you. I do not give peace to you as the world gives. Do not let your hearts be troubled or afraid."

JOHN 14:25–27

Dear Jesus, thank You for sharing this promise with Your disciples that I can believe in today too. I believe God the Father has sent the Holy Spirit to the world in Your place. He is the Helper of all who trust in You as Savior. I believe the Holy Spirit teaches me and guides me and helps me to remember Your truth. I never need to be troubled or afraid, because You are with me every moment through the Holy Spirit, and You give amazing, supernatural peace! Amen.

DAY 5

The Lord Is Near

Those who are right with the Lord cry, and He hears them. And He takes them from all their troubles. The Lord is near to those who have a broken heart. And He saves those who are broken in spirit.

Psalm 34:17–18

Lord, when I'm sad, thank You for hearing my cries. Thank You for staying near to me. Thank You for caring about what makes me sad and wanting to comfort me and help me through it. Sometimes I don't know how to ever feel happy again, but when I think about Your promises to take away my troubles and to save and rescue me, I start to feel better. I'm holding on to You, and You're holding on to me. I love You, Lord! Amen.

DAY 6

Good Words

Worry in the heart. . .weighs it down,
but a good word makes it glad.
Proverbs 12:25

Sometimes worry weighs down my heart and makes me feel heavy and sad and scared, Lord God. In those times, please give me plenty of good words to lift me up and make me glad. Show me which Bible verses I especially need. Help my family and friends to say the things You want me to hear that will help me be happy and brave as I keep trusting in You. Let the songs I hear and sing put my focus on You and fill me with thankfulness and worship. Thank You for showing me Your love and care in both big and little ways! Amen.

DAY 7

As Far as the East Is from the West

His loving-kindness for those who fear Him is as great as the heavens are high above the earth. He has taken our sins from us as far as the east is from the west. The Lord has loving-pity on those who fear Him, as a father has loving-pity on his children.

PSALM 103:11–13

Dear Lord, I made a big mistake, and I'm sorry for my sin. Please forgive me. Please help me to work things out with the people I have hurt. Please help them forgive me too. Thank You that You take away my sins as far as the east is from the west. That's really far away! Your love and mercy are amazing, and I'm thankful! Amen.

DAY 8

The Lord Looks after His People

At my first trial no one helped me. Everyone left me. I hope this will not be held against them. But the Lord was with me. He gave me power to preach the Good News so all the people who do not know God might hear. I was taken from the mouth of the lion. The Lord will look after me and will keep me from every sinful plan they have. He will bring me safe into His holy nation of heaven. May He have all the shining-greatness forever. Let it be so.

2 TIMOTHY 4:16–18

Dear Lord, when I feel all alone and abandoned, remind me that You were with Paul even when everyone else left him. No matter where I go or who is against me, You are standing right by my side, helping me, protecting me, and giving me strength. Amen.

DAY 9

Protected and Ready

Our fight is not with people. It is against the leaders and the powers and the spirits of darkness in this world. It is against the demon world that works in the heavens. Because of this, put on all the things God gives you to fight with. Then you will be able to stand in that sinful day. When it is all over, you will still be standing. So stand up and do not be moved. Wear a belt of truth around your body. Wear a piece of iron over your chest which is being right with God. Wear shoes on your feet which are the Good News of peace. Most important of all, you need a covering of faith in front of you. This is to put out the fire-arrows of the devil. The covering for your head is that you have been saved from the punishment of sin. Take the sword of the Spirit which is the Word of God.

EPHESIANS 6:12–17

Dear Father God, please help me to learn and remember how important it is to be protected and ready with the armor You give to fight the battles against evil in this world. Amen.

DAY 10

God, Who Is Right and Good

Answer me when I call, O my God Who is right and good! You have made a way for me when I needed help. Be kind to me, and hear my prayer.

Psalm 4:1

Dear Lord, You are right and good. Please answer me when I call on You. Help me to remember all the times You have answered me and made a way for me in the past. I trust You will always make a way for me in the future too. Thank You for always being kind to me and for hearing my prayers. I love You! Amen.

DAY 11

Let God Change Your Life

Let your bodies be a living and holy gift given to God. He is pleased with this kind of gift. This is the true worship that you should give Him. Do not act like the sinful people of the world. Let God change your life. First of all, let Him give you a new mind. Then you will know what God wants you to do. And the things you do will be good and pleasing and perfect.

ROMANS 12:1–2

Father God, I am Yours, and I want to live for You! Please change my life to be all about You, because You know what's best! You created me with a purpose and have amazing things in mind for me to do. Help me to think more like You do every day. Please show me Your perfect plans. Amen.

DAY 12

Wisdom Will Come into Your Heart

The Lord gives wisdom. Much learning and understanding come from His mouth. He stores up perfect wisdom for those who are right with Him. He is a safe-covering to those who are right in their walk. He watches over the right way, and He keeps safe the way of those who belong to Him. Then you will understand what is right and good, and right from wrong, and you will know what you should do. For wisdom will come into your heart. And much learning will be pleasing to your soul. Good thinking will keep you safe. Understanding will watch over you.

Proverbs 2:6–11

Dear Lord, I sure do need Your wisdom, and You have promised to give it to me. Help me to know right from wrong. Show me the good things I should do. Help me to stay away from bad thoughts and choices and actions. I believe that when I stick close to You, then I will live in a way that pleases You as You lead me on the path You've mapped out for me. Amen.

DAY 13

What God Wants

Look for ways to do good to each other and to all people. Be full of joy all the time. Never stop praying. In everything give thanks. This is what God wants you to do because of Christ Jesus.

1 Thessalonians 5:15–18

Father God, I should never say I don't know what You want me to do, because Your Word tells me right here in these verses. Please help me to remember this scripture all the time. Help me to constantly be looking for ways to do good to others. Help me to be full of joy every day. Help me to pray and keep on praying! And help me to be thankful for every blessing in my life. Amen.

DAY 14

Even If

Even if the fig tree does not grow figs and there is no fruit on the vines, even if the olives do not grow and the fields give no food, even if there are no sheep within the fence and no cattle in the cattle-building, yet I will have joy in the Lord. I will be glad in the God Who saves me.

Habakkuk 3:17–18

Dear Lord, even if things aren't going my way. . . Even if You don't answer my prayers exactly the way I want. . . Even if I don't understand what You're doing. . . Even if I feel let down again and again, I still want to have joy because You are my Savior. I know You love me, and my hope is in You! Amen.

DAY 15

Together for Good

We know that God makes all things work together for the good of those who love Him and are chosen to be a part of His plan. God knew from the beginning who would put their trust in Him. So He chose them and made them to be like His Son. Christ was first and all those who belong to God are His brothers. He called to Himself also those He chose. Those He called, He made right with Himself. Then He shared His shining-greatness with those He made right with Himself.

ROMANS 8:28–30

Father God, I don't understand how You do it, but I believe that because I love You and have put my trust in You, You make all things (even the bad things going on in my life) work together for good. Thank You! It's amazing that You've known from the very beginning that I would trust in You. Please keep me close to You. I want to please You and be more and more like Jesus every day. Amen.

DAY 16

The Gift of Good Friendship

Two are better than one, because they have good pay for their work. For if one of them falls, the other can help him up. But it is hard for the one who falls when there is no one to lift him up. And if two lie down together, they keep warm. But how can one be warm alone? One man is able to have power over him who is alone, but two can stand against him. It is not easy to break a rope made of three strings.

Ecclesiastes 4:9–12

Dear Lord, thank You for the gift of good friendship. Thank You that my friends and I can support and encourage each other. We can have so much fun too! Show me the best ways I can be a good friend. Help us all to grow closer together and most importantly, closer to You! Amen.

DAY 17

Careful about Friends

He who walks with wise men will be wise, but the one who walks with fools will be destroyed. Trouble follows sinners, but good things will be given to those who are right with God.

PROVERBS 13:20–21

Dear Father God, please help me to be careful about choosing friends. Help me to know the friends You don't want me to have—the ones who will pull me away from obeying You. Help me to show kindness to everyone in my life but to keep my distance from anyone who wants to be mean to me or who could get me into trouble. Please bless me with good, fun friendships, especially friends who encourage me to draw closer to You! Amen.

DAY 18

Power over All through Jesus

What can we say about all these things? Since God is for us, who can be against us? God did not keep His own Son for Himself but gave Him for us all. Then with His Son, will He not give us all things? Who can say anything against the people God has chosen? It is God Who says they are right with Himself. Who then can say we are guilty? It was Christ Jesus Who died. He was raised from the dead. He is on the right side of God praying to Him for us. Who can keep us away from the love of Christ? Can trouble or problems? Can suffering wrong from others or having no food? Can it be because of no clothes or because of danger or war? The Holy Writings say, "Because of belonging to Jesus, we are in danger of being killed all day long. We are thought of as sheep that are ready to be killed." But we have power over all these things through Jesus Who loves us so much.

Romans 8:31–37

Dear Lord, since You are for me, no one can stand a chance against me! Because I am saved through Jesus, no one and nothing can ever keep me away from Your love. Awesome! Amen.

DAY 19

God Did Not Leave Them

"They would not listen, and did not remember Your powerful works which You had done among them. So they became strong-willed and chose a leader to return to their hard work in Egypt. But You are a forgiving God. You are kind and loving, slow to anger, and full of loving-kindness. You did not leave them. They even melted gold and made a calf, and said, 'This is your God Who brought you up from Egypt.' They spoke sinful words against You. But You, in Your great loving-kindness, did not leave them in the desert. The pillar of cloud which led them on their way during the day did not leave them. And the pillar of fire which gave light to the way they were to go during the night did not leave them."

NEHEMIAH 9:17–19

Father God, I'm so thankful for Your mercy. Thank You for loving Your people, including me, so well. Please forgive me when I treat You badly and sin against You. Thank You that You are always willing to forgive me and You never stop loving or providing for me.

DAY 20

Obey God's Word

Obey the Word of God. If you hear only and do not act, you are only fooling yourself. Anyone who hears the Word of God and does not obey is like a man looking at his face in a mirror. After he sees himself and goes away, he forgets what he looks like. But the one who keeps looking into God's perfect Law and does not forget it will do what it says and be happy as he does it. God's Word makes men free.

James 1:22–25

Dear Lord, as I'm growing up, please help me to hear and learn and understand Your Word and obey it. It doesn't mean much if I just hear Your Word and do nothing about it. My obedience to Your Word proves that I love and follow You. It makes me happy and free! I want others to see my love for You and want to know You too. Amen.

DAY 21

God Is There

Where can I go from Your Spirit? Or where can I run away from where You are? If I go up to heaven, You are there! If I make my bed in the place of the dead, You are there! If I take the wings of the morning or live in the farthest part of the sea, even there Your hand will lead me and Your right hand will hold me. If I say, "For sure the darkness will cover me and the light around me will be night," even the darkness is not dark to You. And the night is as bright as the day. Darkness and light are the same to You.

Psalm 139:7–12

Dear Father God, You are everywhere! I never need to be afraid of anything because You are with me no matter where I go or what I'm facing. Your hand leads me and holds me, whether in darkness or daylight. You are my awesome protector and guide. Thank You! Amen.

DAY 22

The Importance of Family

Anyone who does not take care of his family and those in his house has turned away from the faith. He is worse than a person who has never put his trust in Christ.

1 Timothy 5:8

Dear Lord, thank You for my family. We aren't perfect, but we love each other. When we're fighting and upset with each other, please help us to work it out. Help us to forgive and have grace for each other. Help us to take care of each other like we should. May we always serve and honor You. Amen.

DAY 23

Jesus Loves the Little Children

They brought little children to Jesus that He might put His hand on them. The followers spoke sharp words to those who brought them. Jesus saw this and was angry with the followers. He said, "Let the little children come to Me. Do not stop them. The holy nation of God is made up of ones like these. For sure, I tell you, whoever does not receive the holy nation of God as a little child does not go into it." He took the children in His arms. He put His hands on them and prayed that good would come to them.

Mark 10:13–16

Dear Jesus, thank You for loving kids like me so much! You always want kids to come to You. I believe in You and love You with all my heart. As I grow up, help me never to lose my faith and trust in You. Amen.

DAY 24

In the Beginning

In the beginning God made from nothing the heavens and the earth. The earth was an empty waste and darkness was over the deep waters. And the Spirit of God was moving over the top of the waters. Then God said, "Let there be light," and there was light. God saw that the light was good. He divided the light from the darkness. Then God called the light day, and He called the darkness night. There was evening and there was morning, one day.

GENESIS 1:1–5

Father God, I believe in the true story of creation. You made the heavens and earth and everything in them from nothing. You made light. You made day and night. You made the skies and planets and stars. You made plants and trees and every kind of bug and bird and animal. And You made male and female people extra special because people are created in Your image. I believe in You as the one true amazing Creator! Amen.

DAY 25

God Rested

So the heavens and the earth were completed, and all that is in them. On the seventh day God ended His work which He had done. And He rested on the seventh day from all His work which He had done. Then God honored the seventh day and made it holy, because in it He rested from all His work which He had done.

GENESIS 2:1–3

Dear Lord, when You were done creating everything, You rested. And I believe You want me to take time to rest too. Sometimes I don't think resting seems very fun, and sometimes I don't think I need to, but help me remember that rest is good. When I rest, help me to think of You and worship You and spend time praying to You. I want to be close to You, Father. Amen.

DAY 26

Strong and Safe

My soul is quiet and waits for God alone. My hope comes from Him. He alone is my rock and the One Who saves me. He is my strong place. I will not be shaken. My being safe and my honor rest with God. My safe place is in God, the rock of my strength. Trust in Him at all times, O people. Pour out your heart before Him. God is a safe place for us.

Psalm 62:5–8

Dear Father God, thank You for being my rock and the one who saves me. All my hope is in You! You keep me strong and safe. I trust You at all times, and I'm so grateful I can pour out my heart to You. Amen.

DAY 27

Make God Happy

Do not make God's Holy Spirit have sorrow for the way you live. . . . Put out of your life all these things: bad feelings about other people, anger, temper, loud talk, bad talk which hurts other people, and bad feelings which hurt other people. You must be kind to each other. Think of the other person. Forgive other people just as God forgave you because of Christ's death on the cross.

EPHESIANS 4:30–32

Father God, I don't want to make bad choices and make You sad. Please help me to make good choices in my life—choices that show I live to make You happy and give You praise. Help me to get rid of any bad things I do and think. Help me to truly think of other people and love and forgive them in the same way You think of, love, and forgive me. Amen.

DAY 28

The Lord Is Right and Good

The Lord is right and good in all His ways, and kind in all His works. The Lord is near to all who call on Him, to all who call on Him in truth. He will fill the desire of those who fear Him. He will also hear their cry and will save them. The Lord takes care of all who love Him. But He will destroy all the sinful. My mouth will speak the praise of the Lord. And all flesh will honor His holy name forever and ever.

Psalm 145:17–21

Lord, I believe You are right and good in all Your ways and kind in all Your works. Help me to focus on You as I go through any hard time. I will praise and worship You no matter what! You hear my cries and prayers. You will rescue me, bless me, and take care of me. Amen.

DAY 29

God's Powerful Love

Nothing can keep us from the love of God. Death cannot! Life cannot! Angels cannot! Leaders cannot! Any other power cannot! Hard things now or in the future cannot! The world above or the world below cannot! Any other living thing cannot keep us away from the love of God which is ours through Christ Jesus our Lord.

ROMANS 8:38–39

Father God, I feel scared sometimes. When I do, please help me remember that not one thing in this world can ever keep Your love away from me. No matter what big or strong or scary thing I'm facing, it cannot be more powerful than You. Your love for me will always protect me and care for me. Your love for me will aways win. Thank You! Amen.

DAY 30

Speak Truth

The Lord hates lying lips, but those who speak the truth are His joy.
Proverb 12:22

Dear Lord, help me to remember how important the truth is to You. I want to be Your joy! If I'm tempted to tell a lie, please stop me. If I do make a mistake and tell a lie, please help me to confess it quickly and tell the truth. Help me to be trustworthy and honest in everything I do. Being a liar will only bring bad things into my life, but loving the truth and living in truth will bring me many blessings from You! Thank You. Amen.

DAY 31

Look at the Things That Cannot Be Seen

The little troubles we suffer now for a short time are making us ready for the great things God is going to give us forever. We do not look at the things that can be seen. We look at the things that cannot be seen. The things that can be seen will come to an end. But the things that cannot be seen will last forever.

2 Corinthians 4:17–18

Dear Father God, this trouble I'm going through is hard. It seems like it won't end. Help me to keep looking up to You instead of focusing on my problems and troubles. I want to praise and worship You even in the middle of the hard stuff. Help me to have faith in all the good things You are doing that I can't see right now. Amen.

DAY 32

The Lord Is My Shepherd

The Lord is my Shepherd. I will have everything I need. He lets me rest in fields of green grass. He leads me beside the quiet waters. He makes me strong again. He leads me in the way of living right with Himself which brings honor to His name. Yes, even if I walk through the valley of the shadow of death, I will not be afraid of anything, because You are with me. You have a walking stick with which to guide and one with which to help. These comfort me. You are making a table of food ready for me in front of those who hate me. You have poured oil on my head. I have everything I need. For sure, You will give me goodness and loving-kindness all the days of my life. Then I will live with You in Your house forever.

Psalm 23

Dear Lord, I love this scripture. It gives me peace and strength. I feel calm and brave when I read and remember it. Please help me never to forget it, and bring it to mind exactly when I need it. Amen.

DAY 33

Forgiveness

"If you forgive people their sins, your Father in heaven will forgive your sins also. If you do not forgive people their sins, your Father will not forgive your sins."

MATTHEW 6:14–15

Heavenly Father, Your Word has a warning about forgiveness—if I don't forgive others, then You won't forgive me. Please help me to have a lot of grace for others, especially when siblings or friends upset me, and help me to be forgiving toward them. Please show me anywhere I need to give grace and offer forgiveness. Do You see something I'm holding on to that I shouldn't be? Please help me to see it and let go of it and make things right where I can. Amen.

DAY 34

Lots and Lots of Forgiveness

Then Peter came to Jesus and said,
"Lord, how many times may my brother
sin against me and I forgive him, up to
seven times?" Jesus said to him, "I tell you,
not seven times but seventy times seven!"
MATTHEW 18:21–22

Dear Jesus, please help me to really get it—to really know what You meant when You said "not seven times but seventy times seven" when it comes to forgiveness. I want to be full of grace and forgiveness for others just like You are. I'm so glad You don't keep track of how many times I have to ask for forgiveness. If You had a limit, I would be doomed! Please help me to love and forgive like You do. Amen.

DAY 35

God Knows

O Lord, You have looked through me and have known me. You know when I sit down and when I get up. You understand my thoughts from far away. You look over my path and my lying down. You know all my ways very well. Even before I speak a word, O Lord, You know it all. You have closed me in from behind and in front. And You have laid Your hand upon me. All You know is too great for me. It is too much for me to understand.

Psalm 139:1–6

Dear Father God, there is nothing You don't know! Wow! My brain can't really understand that, but that's okay. I don't need to understand everything. I can just keep on trusting in You. I promise to do that, Lord. I believe You are good and that You love and care for me always. Amen.

DAY 36

The Way, the Truth, and the Life

Thomas said to Jesus, "Lord, we do not know where You are going. How can we know the way to get there?" Jesus said, "I am the Way and the Truth and the Life. No one can go to the Father except by Me. If you had known Me, you would know My Father also. From now on you know Him and have seen Him."

JOHN 14:5–7

Dear Jesus, I believe You are the one and only way, truth, and life, just like You told Thomas. Help me to share with others that there is no other way to go to heaven except through You. You are the Holy One of God, and I'm so grateful I know You! Amen.

DAY 37

Weak and Strong

[God] answered me, "I am all you need. I give you My loving-favor. My power works best in weak people." I am happy to be weak and have troubles so I can have Christ's power in me. I receive joy when I am weak. I receive joy when people talk against me and make it hard for me and try to hurt me and make trouble for me. I receive joy when all these things come to me because of Christ. For when I am weak, then I am strong.

2 Corinthians 12:9–10

Dear Father God, please help me to be happy to be weak. The world says I should be strong on my own. But I know my weakness means true strength, because when I am weak I have to depend on Your strength. You are truly all I need, Lord! Make me strong like only You can. Amen.

DAY 38

Jesus Understands

We have a great Religious Leader Who has made the way for man to go to God. He is Jesus, the Son of God, Who has gone to heaven to be with God. Let us keep our trust in Jesus Christ. Our Religious Leader understands how weak we are. Christ was tempted in every way we are tempted, but He did not sin. Let us go with complete trust to the throne of God. We will receive His loving-kindness and have His loving-favor to help us whenever we need it.

HEBREWS 4:14–16

Jesus, remind me that You know what it's like to be human like me because You came to earth as a baby and then grew to be a kid just like me. You struggled and hurt in the same kinds of ways I do, but You never sinned. Wow! And then You died and rose again for my sin, and now You provide the way for me to come to God's throne and receive mercy and grace whenever I need it. I don't deserve Your amazing love, Jesus, but I'm so thankful for it. Amen.

DAY 39

Trust

Show me Your loving-kindness, O God, for man has walked on me. All day long the one who tries to keep me down fights with me. All day long those who hate me have walked on me. For there are many who fight against me with pride. When I am afraid, I will trust in You. I praise the Word of God. I have put my trust in God. I will not be afraid. What can only a man do to me?

Psalm 56:1–4

Dear Lord, I feel like someone is walking all over me too. You know the problem. You know I'm feeling bullied. Please help me. I'm afraid, but I will trust in You. I will praise You and learn from Your Word, no matter what. No one can truly harm me since I have You as my rock and protector. Amen.

DAY 40

Father and Son

"The son got up and went to his father. While he was yet a long way off, his father saw him. The father was full of loving-pity for him. He ran and threw his arms around him and kissed him. The son said to him, 'Father, I have sinned against heaven and against you. I am not good enough to be called your son.' But the father said to the workmen he owned, 'Hurry! Get the best coat and put it on him. Put a ring on his hand and shoes on his feet. Bring the calf that is fat and kill it. Let us eat and be glad. For my son was dead and now he is alive again. He was lost and now he is found. Let us eat and have a good time.'"

LUKE 15:20–24

Dear Father God, thank You for the story of this father and son. It's a picture of Your love. It helps me to know that You love people deeply, no matter what they do. You want to run to those who turn to You—including me—with open arms of forgiveness and love. Thank You! Amen.

DAY 41

Give Your Way to the Lord

Trust in the Lord, and do good. So you will live in the land and will be fed. Be happy in the Lord. And He will give you the desires of your heart. Give your way over to the Lord. Trust in Him also. And He will do it. He will make your being right and good show as the light, and your wise actions as the noon day.

Psalm 37:3–6

Dear Lord, my family is moving and it's hard. I'm scared of everything being different and new. Will I be able to make new friends? Will I find fun new activities to do? Will I miss everything and everyone near my old home too much? I give my way over to You, Father. I trust You to help with all these changes. Amen.

DAY 42

Look for God

"He made from one blood all nations who live on the earth. He set the times and places where they should live. They were to look for God. Then they might feel after Him and find Him because He is not far from each one of us. It is in Him that we live and move and keep on living."

ACTS 17:26–28

Dear Father God, thank You for making me! Thank You for setting the time and place for me to live. I look to You and know You are near. I sense that You are right here with me. In You, I live and move and keep on living. You make me feel loved and protected and brave. Amen.

DAY 43

Testing Your Faith

With this hope you can be happy even if you need to have sorrow and all kinds of tests for awhile. These tests have come to prove your faith and to show that it is good. Gold, which can be destroyed, is tested by fire. Your faith is worth much more than gold and it must be tested also. Then your faith will bring thanks and shining-greatness and honor to Jesus Christ when He comes again. You have never seen Him but you love Him. You cannot see Him now but you are putting your trust in Him. And you have joy so great that words cannot tell about it. You will get what your faith is looking for, which is to be saved from the punishment of sin.

1 Peter 1:6–9

Dear Jesus, remind me that hard times can be tests to see if my faith in You is real and good. I want to pass the tests of my faith with straight As. Even though I can't see You as a person right here beside me, I love You and trust in You no matter what. You are with me through the Holy Spirit, and You fill me with joy! Amen.

DAY 44

Written in Your Book

For You made the parts inside me. You put me together inside my mother. I will give thanks to You, for the greatness of the way I was made brings fear. Your works are great and my soul knows it very well. My bones were not hidden from You when I was made in secret and put together with care in the deep part of the earth. Your eyes saw me before I was put together. And all the days of my life were written in Your book before any of them came to be.

Psalm 139:13–16

Wow, Lord, You sure do know and love me! You made me in such an awesome way. I trust that You know every single day of my life from beginning to end. You watch over me and care for me and have great plans for me. I'm so thankful, and I love You! Amen.

DAY 45

Let Good Have Power

"If the one who hates you is hungry, feed him. If he is thirsty, give him water. If you do that, you will be making him more ashamed of himself." Do not let sin have power over you. Let good have power over sin!
ROMANS 12:20–21

Dear Father God, help me to do good to others even if they're being mean to me. I don't really want to do this on my own. I can only do it with Your strength and Your love working in me. When I obey You in this way, You help those who are being mean realize they should be ashamed of themselves for acting badly. Help me to remember not to let sin have power over me. I want to let good have power over sin! Amen.

DAY 46

At All Times

I will honor the Lord at all times. His praise will always be in my mouth. My soul will be proud to tell about the Lord. Let those who suffer hear it and be filled with joy. Give great honor to the Lord with me. Let us praise His name together. I looked for the Lord, and He answered me. And He took away all my fears.

Psalm 34:1–4

Dear Lord, these verses show me how I can rise above fear. If I'm praising You and telling others about You at all times, there won't be room in my mind for fears. When I look for You and think of all the reasons to worship You, I won't be afraid because I'll be focused on how great and mighty and awesome and powerful You are. It's a win-win! Thank You! Amen.

DAY 47

The Holy Spirit Prays

In the same way, the Holy Spirit helps us where we are weak. We do not know how to pray or what we should pray for, but the Holy Spirit prays to God for us with sounds that cannot be put into words. God knows the hearts of men. He knows what the Holy Spirit is thinking. The Holy Spirit prays for those who belong to Christ the way God wants Him to pray.

ROMANS 8:26–27

Father God, when I'm feeling so weak and helpless that I don't even know what to pray, remind me that the Holy Spirit is praying to You for me. The Spirit helps me in my weakness. You know what's in my heart and what I need. Thank You so much for loving and caring for me so well. Amen.

DAY 48

Because You Are Young

Tell people that this is what they must do.
Let no one show little respect for you because
you are young. Show other Christians how to
live by your life. They should be able to follow
you in the way you talk and in what you do.
Show them how to live in faith and in love and
in holy living. Until I come, read and preach
and teach the Word of God to the church.
Be sure to use the gift God gave you.

1 Timothy 4:11–14

Dear Father God, help me never to think that I don't matter much or can't do much just because I'm young. I can do awesome things to help share Your truth and love with others. You have good plans for me—not just when I grow up, but right now and every day of my life. Please lead me and guide me in those good things. Amen.

DAY 49

A Glad Heart

A glad heart is good medicine,
but a broken spirit dries up the bones.
PROVERBS 17:22

Dear Jesus, I'm so glad You want me to be happy and cheerful! The best kind of happy comes from knowing You are my Savior from sin and nothing can ever take Your love away from me. Anytime I feel sad about anything, help me to cheer right back up again when I remember the awesome hope that I have in You! Help me to happily shine the light of Your love and hope to others. Help me to always have and always be sharing the good medicine of a glad heart that comes from knowing You! Amen.

DAY 50

Wait for the Lord

I would have been without hope if I had not believed that I would see the loving-kindness of the Lord in the land of the living. Wait for the Lord. Be strong. Let your heart be strong. Yes, wait for the Lord.

Psalm 27:13–14

Dear Lord, I don't really like to wait. I get very impatient. I want what I want right away. But that's not always right, and You don't always want that for me. Sometimes You want me to be patient and wait with a good attitude. Help me to be a good waiter and to remember that You have good things You want me to learn during the waiting time. Please help me to be strong and full of hope and joy while I wait.

DAY 51

Prayers for Friends and Loved Ones

Dear friend, I pray that you are doing well in every way. I pray that your body is strong and well even as your soul is. I was very happy when some Christians came and told me about how you are following the truth. I can have no greater joy than to hear that my children are following the truth.

3 John 1:2–4

Dear Father God, thank You for my friends and loved ones! I pray the prayer of this scripture for them. Help them to be doing well in every way. Help them to be strong in both body and soul. I pray that they know and follow the truth found in Your Word. I pray that they trust in Jesus as their Savior. Amen.

DAY 52

Live in Peace

When someone does something bad to you,
do not pay him back with something bad.
Try to do what all men know is right and good.
As much as you can, live in peace with all men.
Christian brothers, never pay back someone
for the bad he has done to you. Let the anger
of God take care of the other person.

ROMANS 12:17–19

Dear Lord, it's so hard not to be mean when others are being mean to me! I want to pay them back what they deserve. I need a lot of help to obey Your Word and let You take care of it. You know what happened, and You will make things right. Help me to live in peace, doing what is right and good, just like You ask me to. Amen.

DAY 53

The Many Things Jesus Did

This is the follower who is telling of these things and who has written them. We know that his word is true. There are many other things which Jesus did also. If they were all written down, I do not think the world itself could hold the books that would be written.

JOHN 21:24–25

Dear Jesus, this scripture is so cool! When I think about all the miracles You did when You lived on earth, I'm amazed. Help me to think of how awesome You are whenever I'm feeling sad or helpless. You can do absolutely anything to encourage me and come to my rescue. I'm so grateful You are my Savior and friend! Amen.

DAY 54

Don't Trouble Yourself

Rest in the Lord and be willing to wait for Him. Do not trouble yourself when all goes well with the one who carries out his sinful plans. Stop being angry. Turn away from fighting. Do not trouble yourself. It leads only to wrong-doing. For those who do wrong will be cut off. But those who wait for the Lord will be given the earth.

Psalm 37:7–9

Father God, I get frustrated when those who cheat or do other bad things seem to have everything go well for them. But Your Word tells me not to worry about that. Help me to focus on my own actions. Help me to keep obeying and following You. Help me not to be angry and sin. You will deal with those who do wrong, and You will bless those who do right. Amen.

DAY 55

The Secret of Being Happy

I have learned to be happy with whatever I have. I know how to get along with little and how to live when I have much. I have learned the secret of being happy at all times. If I am full of food and have all I need, I am happy. If I am hungry and need more, I am happy. I can do all things because Christ gives me the strength.

PHILIPPIANS 4:11–13

Dear Lord, help me to remember how to be happy at all times—by trusting in You whether I have a lot or a little. You know exactly what I truly need, and You will always provide everything I truly need. What's more, You promise to give me strength when I need it. You *are* my strength when I need it. I can do anything at all because You love me and are with me. Amen.

DAY 56

The Earth Is the Lord's

The earth is the Lord's, and all that is in it, the world, and all who live in it. For He has built it upon the seas. He has set it upon the rivers. Who may go up the mountain of the Lord? And who may stand in His holy place? He who has clean hands and a pure heart. He who has not lifted up his soul to what is not true, and has not made false promises. He will receive what is good from the Lord, and what is right and good from the God Who saves him.

Psalm 24:1–5

Dear Father God, everything in the earth is Yours! *Everything*, including me. You have created it all, and You sustain it all. You rule over the whole cosmos as the one true King. How grateful I am to be known and loved by You! Amen.

DAY 57

Loving God's Word

O, how I love Your Law! It is what I think about all through the day. Your Word makes me wiser than those who hate me, for it is always with me. I have better understanding than all my teachers because I think about Your Law. I have a better understanding than those who are old because I obey Your Word. I have kept my feet from every sinful way so that I may keep Your Word. I have not turned away from Your Law, for You Yourself have taught me. How sweet is Your Word to my taste! It is sweeter than honey to my mouth! I get understanding from Your Law and so I hate every false way.

Psalm 119:97–104

Dear Lord, I want this psalm to be true about me. Help me to love Your Word so, so, so much! Give me a longing to read and learn from it all the time. I know it will bring me closer to You and help me live the best kind of life. Amen.

DAY 58

Rest for Your Soul

"Come to Me, all of you who work and have heavy loads. I will give you rest. Follow My teachings and learn from Me. I am gentle and do not have pride. You will have rest for your souls. For My way of carrying a load is easy and My load is not heavy."

Matthew 11:28–30

Father God, I feel stressed out by everything going on in my life. With homework and activities and chores and friends and family, I have a lot to do! Please help me not to worry or feel anxious or tired in the middle of it all. Please help me to be wise with my time. Most of all, please help me to live for You and find the rest and peace I need in You. Amen.

DAY 59

No Big Words Needed

Christ. . .sent me to preach the Good News. I did not use big sounding words when I preached. If I had, the power of the cross of Christ would be taken away.

1 Corinthians 1:17

Dear Jesus, help me remember that if You didn't expect the apostle Paul to use big-sounding words to share Your good news, You sure don't expect me to either. I shouldn't think I'm just a kid who can't teach others about You. I shouldn't think I'm too young. I can share in whatever ways You lead me to share, whenever and wherever You show me. I just want the awesome power of the truth about Your work on the cross to be what makes a big impact on people. Amen.

DAY 60

The Right Thing to Do

Children, as Christians, obey your parents. This is the right thing to do. Respect your father and mother. This is the first Law given that had a promise. The promise is this: If you respect your father and mother, you will live a long time and your life will be full of many good things.

EPHESIANS 6:1–3

Father God, I don't always obey and respect my parents. And sometimes even when I do, I'm not very happy about it. Please forgive me and help me. Remind me that I'm obeying and honoring You when I obey and respect my parents. Please help me to obey and respect with a good attitude, not in rude and grumpy ways. Please bless me as I obey with a cheerful and thankful heart. Amen.

DAY 61

Feeling Betrayed

When Jesus had said this, He was troubled in heart. He told them in very plain words, saying, "For sure, I tell you, one of you is going to hand Me over to the leaders of the country." . . . While close beside Jesus, [the follower whom Jesus loved] asked, "Lord, who is it?" Jesus answered, "It is the one I give this piece of bread to after I have put it in the dish." Then He put the bread in the dish and gave it to Judas Iscariot, the son of Simon. After Judas had eaten the piece of bread, Satan went into him. Jesus said to Judas, "What you are going to do, do in a hurry."

John 13:21, 25–27

Jesus, someone I thought was a good friend has totally turned on me. This "friend" is so mean to me! You were betrayed by Your friend Judas in the worst kind of way, so I know You understand how I'm feeling. I'm sorry Judas turned his back on You, but I also know God was working good things in the middle of Your betrayal. Please work good things for me too. I trust You will. Thank You! Amen.

DAY 62

Strong and Free

O Lord, in You I have found a safe place.
Let me never be ashamed. Set me free,
because You do what is right and good.
Turn Your ear to me, and be quick to save me.
Be my rock of strength, a strong place to keep
me safe. For You are my rock and my safe
place. For the honor of Your name, lead me and
show me the way. You will free me from the net
that they have hidden for me. For You are my
strength. I give my spirit into Your hands.
You have made me free, O Lord, God of truth.

PSALM 31:1–5

Lord, I pray this scripture to You. You are my rock and my safe place. You are my strength and truth. I am saved and free because of You! Thank You! Amen.

DAY 63

Truly Free

Obey the head leader of the country and all other leaders over you. This pleases the Lord. Obey the men who work for them. God sends them to punish those who do wrong and to show respect to those who do right. This is what God wants. When you do right, you stop foolish men from saying bad things. Obey as men who are free but do not use this to cover up sin. Live as servants owned by God at all times. Show respect to all men. Love the Christians. Honor God with love and fear. Respect the head leader of the country.

1 Peter 2:13–17

Dear Father God, please help me to be a good and respectful citizen of my country who shines Your light of love and truth through my behavior. I know I am truly free in You no matter what country I live in. Amen.

DAY 64

Whoever Obeys

We can be sure that we know Him if we obey His teaching. Anyone who says, "I know Him," but does not obey His teaching is a liar. There is no truth in him. But whoever obeys His Word has the love of God made perfect in him. This is the way to know if you belong to Christ. The one who says he belongs to Christ should live the same kind of life Christ lived.

1 John 2:3–6

Dear Jesus, I want to show others that I truly know You, and I can do that by obeying Your teaching and living the same kind of life You did. But I can't really live the way You did unless I read and learn about You in Your Word. Help me to recognize who truly knows You as Savior and who doesn't by seeing whether they obey Your teaching and live like You or not. Amen.

DAY 65

Weak from Being Sad

Show me loving-kindness, O Lord, for I am in trouble. My eyes, my soul and my body are becoming weak from being sad. For my life gets weaker with sorrow, and my years with crying inside myself.

PSALM 31:9–10

Father God, I know what it's like to feel in trouble and sad like this scripture describes. Please show me Your love in many different ways during those times. Help me to trust that You see and care about every tear I cry. You will help me in my sadness. You will help make things right. Please keep me close to You as I wait for things to get better. Amen.

DAY 66

God's Good Plans

" 'For I know the plans I have for you,' says the Lord, 'plans for well-being and not for trouble, to give you a future and a hope. Then you will call upon Me and come and pray to Me, and I will listen to you. You will look for Me and find Me, when you look for Me with all your heart.' "

JEREMIAH 29:11–13

Dear Lord, I believe You have good plans for me. Please show them to me every day. I believe You have a future of blessing and hope in store for me. I want to follow and serve You. I trust You will listen when I pray, and I trust I will find You when I look for You with all my heart. Amen.

DAY 67

Everything to Honor God

Whatever you do, do everything to honor God.
1 CORINTHIANS 10:31

Dear Father God, help me to remember this verse every minute of every day. I can choose to do everything in a way that honors You. I can worship and give thanks for all the things I'm capable of. I can have a good attitude even while doing schoolwork and chores. I can use the special talents and gifts You've given me to do the good works You've created me for. In everything I accomplish, I can praise You and give You glory. I can tell others that You are the reason for my gifts and my joy and my hard work and my abilities. I can do awesome things because You are awesome within me, Lord! Thank You! Amen.

DAY 68

A Covering

You, O Lord, are a covering around me,
my shining-greatness, and the One Who lifts
my head. I was crying to the Lord with my voice.
And He answered me from His holy mountain.
I lay down and slept, and I woke up again,
for the Lord keeps me safe. I will not be afraid of
ten thousands of people who stand all around
against me. Rise up, O Lord! Save me, O my God!
PSALM 3:3–7

Dear Lord, when I'm scared, help me to picture You as a covering around me. There is no better protective shield than You! You lift my head when I'm feeling sad and worried. You hear and answer me when I cry. You give me peace and restful sleep. No matter who or what is against me, I don't need to be afraid. Amen.

DAY 69

Your Shepherd

[Jesus] never sinned. No lie or bad talk ever came from His lips. When people spoke against Him, He never spoke back. When He suffered from what people did to Him, He did not try to pay them back. He left it in the hands of the One Who is always right in judging. He carried our sins in His own body when He died on a cross. In doing this, we may be dead to sin and alive to all that is right and good. His wounds have healed you! You were like lost sheep. But now you have come back to Him Who is your Shepherd and the One Who cares for your soul.

1 PETER 2:22–25

Dear Jesus, You are the best example for me to follow. Help me to be more like You. You saved me and You love me. You are my Shepherd and the one who cares for my soul. Amen.

DAY 70

The One Who Keeps You from Falling

There is One Who can keep you from falling and can bring you before Himself free from all sin. He can give you great joy as you stand before Him in His shining-greatness. He is the only God. He is the One Who saves from the punishment of sin through Jesus Christ our Lord. May He have shining-greatness and honor and power and the right to do all things. He had this before the world began, He has it now, and He will have this forever.

Jude 1:24–25

Dear Father God, You are the one who can keep me from falling and failing in this life. You give me so much joy as I stand before You without fear because of what Jesus did for me. You save me from the punishment of sin through Jesus, whom You sent to take that punishment in my place. I honor You and love You forever and ever! Amen.

DAY 71

Right with God

If Abraham was made right with God by what he did, he would have had something to be proud of. But he could not be proud before God. The Holy Writings say, "Abraham put his trust in God and that made him right with God." If a man works, his pay is not a gift. It is something he has earned. If a man has not worked to be saved, but has put his trust in God Who saves men from the punishment of their sins, that man is made right with God because of his trust in God.

Romans 4:2–5

Dear Father God, nothing I've done or can do will make me right with You. Righteousness is all about what You did by sending Your Son, Jesus, to die for the punishment of my sin. It's because I believe in You and in Jesus' work on the cross that I am saved from sin and made right with You. Thank You for such awesome gifts of grace and faith. Amen.

DAY 72

Sing with Joy Forever

Let all who put their trust in You be glad.
Let them sing with joy forever. You make a
covering for them, that all who love Your name
may be glad in You. For You will make those
happy who do what is right, O Lord. You will
cover them all around with Your favor.

Psalm 5:11–12

Dear Lord, I can be glad every day because I put my trust in You! I can sing with joy forever. You are always protecting me and blessing me. Let other people see my joy, and help me to share with them why I'm so joyful—because You love me and You are my Savior. Thank You!

DAY 73

The Lord Keeps His Promises

Dear friends, remember this one thing, with the Lord one day is as 1,000 years, and 1,000 years are as one day. The Lord is not slow about keeping His promise as some people think. He is waiting for you. The Lord does not want any person to be punished forever. He wants all people to be sorry for their sins and turn from them.

2 Peter 3:8–9

Dear Lord, sometimes it seems like we've been waiting forever for You to come back to earth and make all Your promises come true. Help me to remember that the way I view time is not the way You view time. You are patient and loving. You want all people to be sorry for their sins so You can save them. Help me to want that too, and give me boldness to share the good news of Jesus so that others might believe in You! Amen.

DAY 74

Show Love by What We Do

What if a person has enough money to live on and sees his brother in need of food and clothing? If he does not help him, how can the love of God be in him? My children, let us not love with words or in talk only. Let us love by what we do and in truth.

1 John 3:17–18

Dear Jesus, please help me to notice those who are in need around me. Help me never to ignore them. Show me how You want me to help. Let me get others involved in helping too. I know I can't just say I love You and not show love to others. I need to show my love for You through what I do and how I help. Amen.

DAY 75

Fish for Men

Jesus was walking by the Sea of Galilee. He saw two brothers. They were Simon (his other name was Peter) and Andrew, his brother. They were putting a net into the sea for they were fishermen. Jesus said to them, "Follow Me. I will make you fish for men!" At once they left their nets and followed Him. Going from there, Jesus saw two other brothers. They were James and John, the sons of Zebedee. They were sitting in a boat with their father, mending their nets. Jesus called them. At once they left the boat and their father and followed Jesus.

MATTHEW 4:18–22

Dear Jesus, I want to be like Your friends the disciples. When You called them, they came right away. They wanted to follow You and fish for men—they wanted to help more people know and love and follow You. Please use me to help more people follow You too. Amen.

DAY 76

God Is Light

God is light. There is no darkness in Him. If we say we are joined together with Him but live in darkness, we are telling a lie. We are not living the truth. If we live in the light as He is in the light, we share what we have in God with each other. And the blood of Jesus Christ, His Son, makes our lives clean from all sin. If we say that we have no sin, we lie to ourselves and the truth is not in us. If we tell Him our sins, He is faithful and we can depend on Him to forgive us of our sins. He will make our lives clean from all sin. If we say we have not sinned, we make God a liar. And His Word is not in our hearts.

1 John 1:5–10

Dear Father God, You are light, and I want to live in Your light. I want no part of darkness, and I want to be washed clean from all my sin. I confess my sins to You, and I trust that You forgive them. Please keep filling my heart with Your Word. Amen.

DAY 77

Don't Be Led Away

Watch so you will not be led away by the mistakes of these sinful people. Do not be moved by them. Grow in the loving-favor that Christ gives you. Learn to know our Lord Jesus Christ better. He is the One Who saves. May He have all the shining-greatness now and forever. Let it be so.

2 Peter 3:17–18

Dear Jesus, please help me to be careful that sinful people don't ever lead me away from You. Give me wisdom. Help me to see who tells the truth and who tells lies. Bring people into my life who truly love and follow You and won't lead me away from You. Keep me growing closer and closer to You, learning more about You and growing stronger in Your Word every day.

DAY 78

Don't Give Up on Doing Good

If a man does things to please the Holy Spirit, he will have life that lasts forever. Do not let yourselves get tired of doing good. If we do not give up, we will get what is coming to us at the right time. Because of this, we should do good to everyone. For sure, we should do good to those who belong to Christ.

Galatians 6:8–10

Father God, I see some kids doing wrong things and never getting in trouble for them, so sometimes I get tired of doing the right thing—especially if it seems like it doesn't matter. Please help me not to be discouraged. Help me not to give up on doing good works and doing good to others. No matter what anyone else is doing, I want to make You happy with my life and actions. Amen.

DAY 79

Chosen to Belong

The Holy Spirit proved by a powerful act that Jesus our Lord is the Son of God because He was raised from the dead. Jesus has given us His loving-favor and has made us His missionaries. We are to preach to the people of all nations that they should obey Him and put their trust in Him. You have been chosen to belong to Jesus Christ also. So I write to all of you in the city of Rome. God loves you and has chosen you to be set apart for Himself. May God our Father and the Lord Jesus Christ give you His loving-favor and peace.

ROMANS 1:4–7

Dear Jesus, I believe You died and rose again to save people from their sin. I have been chosen to belong to You. You have given me Your loving-favor, and I am Your missionary. Help me to be brave in telling others that they should obey You and put their trust in You too. Amen.

DAY 80

My Cries for Help

I am tired of crying inside myself. All night long my pillow is wet with tears. I flood my bed with them. My eye has grown weak with sorrow. It has grown old because of all who hate me. Go away from me, all you who sin. For the Lord has heard the sound of my crying. The Lord has heard my cry for help. The Lord receives my prayer. All those who hate me will be ashamed and worried. They will turn away. They will be put to shame right away.

Psalm 6:6–10

Dear Lord, I'm so sad and have so many tears just like this scripture describes. Please help me. You know my troubles and why I'm crying so much. I believe You hear my prayer. I believe You will stop those who are hurting me and causing me trouble, and You will bring about justice. Amen.

DAY 81

Healing and Helping

Jesus went over all Galilee. He taught in their places of worship and preached the Good News of the holy nation. He healed all kinds of sickness and disease among the people. The news about Him went over all the country of Syria. They brought all the sick people to Him with many kinds of diseases and pains. They brought to Him those who had demons. They brought those who at times lose the use of their minds. They brought those who could not use their hands and legs. He healed them.

Matthew 4:23–24

Dear Jesus, You can heal and help anyone. You are amazing. Watching You teach and take care of people while You were here on earth must have been so cool. I know You are still here through the Holy Spirit today, and I believe You are still working in awesome ways every day to heal and to help. Amen.

DAY 82

Trust in the Name of Jesus

Put your trust in the name of His Son, Jesus Christ, and love each other. Christ told us to do this. The person who obeys Christ lives by the help of God and God lives in him. We know He lives in us by the Holy Spirit He has given us.

1 John 3:23–24

Father God, I put all my trust in the name of Your Son, Jesus Christ! Help me to love others well. I want to obey Jesus, and I believe I can do that through the help of Your Holy Spirit living in me. No matter what I need or what trouble or problem I'm facing, I can ask Your Holy Spirit to help me, to give me wisdom, to provide for me, and to protect me. Thank You! Amen.

DAY 83

Do What Is Good

Love each other with a kind heart and with a mind that has no pride. When someone does something bad to you, do not do the same thing to him. When someone talks about you, do not talk about him. Instead, pray that good will come to him. You were called to do this so you might receive good things from God. For "If you want joy in your life and have happy days, keep your tongue from saying bad things and your lips from talking bad about others. Turn away from what is sinful. Do what is good. Look for peace and go after it."

1 Peter 3:8–11

Dear Jesus, please forgive me when I don't obey this scripture. It's so hard to keep from doing something bad back when someone does something bad to me first. But that's not what You want me to do. When a friend or classmate or sibling treats me in a bad way, please help me to pray for them instead of repay them. I can only do what is good with Your help and Your great big love flowing through me. Amen.

DAY 84

Be Salt and Light

"You are the salt of the earth. If salt loses its taste, how can it be made to taste like salt again? It is no good. It is thrown away and people walk on it. You are the light of the world. You cannot hide a city that is on a mountain. Men do not light a lamp and put it under a basket. They put it on a table so it gives light to all in the house. Let your light shine in front of men. Then they will see the good things you do and will honor your Father Who is in heaven."

MATTHEW 5:13–16

Dear Jesus, please help me to be salt and light in the world. I want people to see a good difference in me because I love and follow You. I want to shine brightly with Your truth and love and help point other people to You so they can love and follow You too. Amen.

DAY 85

Jesus Washed Their Feet

Jesus got up from the supper and took off His coat. He picked up a cloth and put it around Him. Then He put water into a wash pan and began to wash the feet of His followers. He dried their feet with the cloth He had put around Himself. Jesus came to Simon Peter. Peter said to Him, "Lord, are You going to wash my feet?" Jesus answered him, "You do not understand now what I am doing but you will later." Peter said to Him, "I will never let You wash my feet." Jesus said, "Unless I wash you, you will not be a part of Me." Simon Peter said to Him, "Lord, do not wash only my feet, but wash my hands and my head also."

John 13:4–9

Jesus, You are the King of all kings, yet You served others so compassionately, even washing Your followers' feet. I want to be a humble, compassionate servant like You. And I want to be like Peter who loved You so much. Amen.

DAY 86

Able to Speak in Other Languages

The followers of Jesus were all together in one place fifty days after the special religious gathering to remember how the Jews left Egypt. All at once there was a sound from heaven like a powerful wind. It filled the house where they were sitting. Then they saw tongues which were divided that looked like fire. These came down on each one of them. They were all filled with the Holy Spirit. Then they began to speak in other languages which the Holy Spirit made them able to speak.

Acts 2:1–4

Dear Jesus, I'm amazed when I read that Your followers were filled with the Holy Spirit and then were able to speak in other languages! You want everyone to be able to hear and know about the good news that You died on the cross and rose again to save people from their sin and give them eternal life. You can do anything to help people share Your good news! You are awesome! Amen.

DAY 87

Because Love Comes from God

Dear friends, let us love each other, because love comes from God. Those who love are God's children and they know God. Those who do not love do not know God because God is love. God has shown His love to us by sending His only Son into the world. God did this so we might have life through Christ. This is love! It is not that we loved God but that He loved us. For God sent His Son to pay for our sins with His own blood. Dear friends, if God loved us that much, then we should love each other. No person has ever seen God at any time. If we love each other, God lives in us. His love is made perfect in us. He has given us His Spirit. This is how we live by His help and He lives in us.

1 John 4:7–13

Dear Father God, please help me to keep learning about Your love and ways that I can share it with others. Help all of us who believe in You to truly love one another. Amen.

DAY 88

Jesus Cried

Mary went to the place where Jesus was. When she saw Him, she got down at His feet. She said to Him, "Lord, if You had been here, my brother would not have died." Jesus saw her crying. The Jews who came with her were crying also. His heart was very sad and He was troubled. He said, "Where did you lay Lazarus?" They said, "Lord, come and see." Then Jesus cried. The Jews said, "See how much He loved Lazarus."

John 11:32–36

Dear Jesus, You knew what it was like to have good friends here on earth. And You know how sad it is when someone we love dies. You have compassion, and You provided the way for all people to have eternal life if they admit their sin and believe in You as their Savior from sin. Thank You, thank You, thank You! Amen.

DAY 89

Treasures in Heaven

"Do not gather together for yourself riches of this earth. They will be eaten by bugs and become rusted. Men can break in and steal them. Gather together riches in heaven where they will not be eaten by bugs or become rusted. Men cannot break in and steal them. For wherever your riches are, your heart will be there also."

MATTHEW 6:19–21

Dear Jesus, help me to realize what true riches are—the ones that are stored up in heaven for me. True riches aren't dollars and cents and the things we can buy here on earth. You reserve true riches that last forever for those who follow and obey You, who serve You and others, who give generously and take care of others' needs. What a beautiful life You want me to live and then bless me for in heaven. Amen.

DAY 90

Real, True Love

Love does not give up. Love is kind. Love is not jealous. Love does not put itself up as being important. Love has no pride. Love does not do the wrong thing. Love never thinks of itself. Love does not get angry. Love does not remember the suffering that comes from being hurt by someone. Love is not happy with sin. Love is happy with the truth. Love takes everything that comes without giving up. Love believes all things. Love hopes for all things. Love keeps on in all things. Love never comes to an end.

1 Corinthians 13:4–8

Dear Father God, the world tries to tell me a lot of things about what love is, but You are the Creator of all things, including love. You are love itself, and we love because You first loved us. Every true thing about love is what Your Word, the Bible, teaches about love. Help me to keep learning about and growing in Your real love. Amen.

DAY 91

The Most High

I will give thanks to the Lord with all my heart. I will tell of all the great things You have done. I will be glad and full of joy because of You. I will sing praise to Your name, O Most High.

Psalm 9:1–2

Dear Lord, help me to remember this scripture. I want it to be true of me. I want to give thanks to You always with all my heart. I want to tell others of all the great things You have done. I want to be glad and full of joy because of You. I want to sing praise to Your name because You are the Most High! Amen.

DAY 92

Walking on the Water

Just before the light of day, Jesus went to them walking on the water. When the followers saw Him walking on the water, they were afraid. They said, "It is a spirit." They cried out with fear. At once Jesus spoke to them and said, "Take hope. It is I. Do not be afraid!" Peter said to Jesus, "If it is You, Lord, tell me to come to You on the water." Jesus said, "Come!" Peter got out of the boat and walked on the water to Jesus. But when he saw the strong wind, he was afraid. He began to go down in the water. He cried out, "Lord, save me!" At once Jesus put out His hand and took hold of him. Jesus said to Peter, "You have so little faith! Why did you doubt?"

MATTHEW 14:25–31

Dear Jesus, seeing You walk on water must have been so cool. I want to be brave like Peter, who wanted to walk on water too. But help me not to doubt and sink down into the water. Help me to keep my faith in You! Amen.

DAY 93

The First Church

They were faithful in listening to the teaching of the missionaries. They worshiped and prayed and ate the Lord's supper together. Many powerful works were done by the missionaries. Surprise and fear came on them all. All those who put their trust in Christ were together and shared what they owned. As anyone had need, they sold what they owned and shared with everyone. Day after day they went to the house of God together. In their houses they ate their food together. Their hearts were happy. They gave thanks to God and all the people respected them. The Lord added to the group each day those who were being saved from the punishment of sin.

Acts 2:42–47

Father God, thank You for the example of the first church. Please help my church to be like they were. Show me how You want me to carry out my part in the church too. Amen.

DAY 94

Not Hard to Obey

Loving God means to obey His Word, and His Word is not hard to obey. Every child of God has power over the sins of the world. The way we have power over the sins of the world is by our faith. Who could have power over the world except by believing that Jesus is the Son of God?

1 John 5:3–5

Dear Lord, when I feel like obeying Your Word is just too hard, please remind me that it's not. You have given me power over the sin of this world because I believe that Jesus is Your Son and that He died and rose again to save all people from their sin. So every time I'm tempted to disobey You, I just need to remember Your power within me. I trust that You will help me obey. Amen.

DAY 95

Ask, Look, Knock

"Ask, and what you are asking for will be given to you. Look, and what you are looking for you will find. Knock, and the door you are knocking on will be opened to you. Everyone who asks receives what he asks for. Everyone who looks finds what he is looking for. Everyone who knocks has the door opened to him. What man among you would give his son a stone if he should ask for bread? Or if he asks for a fish, would he give him a snake? You are bad and you know how to give good things to your children. How much more will your Father in heaven give good things to those who ask Him?"

MATTHEW 7:7–11

Dear Jesus, please keep teaching me about prayer. Help me to ask, look, and knock in ways that match what You want for me. You love to give me good things, and I'm so grateful! Amen.

DAY 96

Do You Believe This?

Martha heard that Jesus was coming and went to meet Him. Mary stayed in the house. Martha said to Jesus, "Lord, if You had been here, my brother would not have died. I know even now God will give You whatever You ask." Jesus said to her, "Your brother will rise again." Martha said to Him, "I know that he will rise again when the dead are raised from the grave on the last day." Jesus said to her, "I am the One Who raises the dead and gives them life. Anyone who puts his trust in Me will live again, even if he dies. Anyone who lives and has put his trust in Me will never die. Do you believe this?" She answered, "Yes, Lord, I believe that You are the Christ, the Son of God. You are the One Who was to come into the world."

JOHN 11:20–27

Dear Jesus, I do believe You, and I'm so grateful for Your promise that anyone who puts their trust in You will live again, even if they die here on earth. Help me to share this truth with others. You are our one true hope, Jesus! Amen.

DAY 97

Angels

Are not all the angels spirits who work for God?
They are sent out to help those who are to
be saved from the punishment of sin.

Hebrews 1:14

Dear Father God, thank You for Your angels. They are spirits who work for You to help all of us who belong to You because we believe in Jesus as our Savior. Your Word says You will tell Your angels to care for me and keep me in all my ways. They will hold me up in their hands (Psalm 91:11–12). Even if I can't see them, I'm so thankful for the ways Your angels protect and watch out for me. I can only imagine how they might be helping me even right this very moment! Your care for me is awesome! Amen.

DAY 98

The One Who Turned Back

Jesus went on His way to Jerusalem. He was passing between the countries of Samaria and Galilee. As He was going into one of the towns, ten men with a bad skin disease came to Him. They stood a little way off. They called to Him, "Jesus! Teacher! Take pity on us!" When Jesus saw them, He said, "Go and show yourselves to the religious leaders." As they went, they were healed. One of them turned back when he saw he was healed. He thanked God with a loud voice. He got down on his face at the feet of Jesus and thanked Him. He was from the country of Samaria. Jesus asked, "Were there not ten men who were healed? Where are the other nine? Is this stranger from another country the only one who turned back to give thanks to God?" Then Jesus said to him, "Get up and go on your way. Your trust in God has healed you."

LUKE 17:11–19

Dear Jesus, I always want to be like the one man who turned back to thank You for healing him. I never want to forget to show my gratitude to You! Amen.

DAY 99

Great Is God's Name in All the Earth

When I look up and think about Your heavens, the work of Your fingers, the moon and the stars, which You have set in their place, what is man, that You think of him, the son of man that You care for him? You made him a little less than the angels and gave him a crown of greatness and honor. You made him to rule over the works of Your hands. You put all things under his feet: All sheep and cattle, all the wild animals, the birds of the air, and the fish of the sea, and all that pass through the sea. O Lord, our Lord, how great is Your name in all the earth!

Psalm 8:3–9

Dear Lord, when I look up at the night sky, I'm amazed. You are so big and awesome—the one true Creator God. You are great and worthy of all my praise! Amen.

DAY 100

Watch Out

"Watch out for false teachers. They come to you dressed as if they were sheep. On the inside they are hungry wolves. You will know them by their fruit. Do men pick grapes from thorns? Do men pick figs from thistles? It is true, every good tree has good fruit. Every bad tree has bad fruit. A good tree cannot have bad fruit. A bad tree cannot have good fruit. Every tree that does not have good fruit is cut down and thrown into the fire. So you will know them by their fruit."

MATTHEW 7:15–20

Dear Jesus, help me to watch out for false teachers who want to lead me away from You. They can be so tricky, looking nice and tame like sheep on the outside but actually being dangerous like wolves on the inside. Help me to see by their fruit, meaning the things they do, whether people are good or bad. Amen.

DAY 101

Run the Race

You know that only one person gets a crown for being in a race even if many people run. You must run so you will win the crown. Everyone who runs in a race does many things so his body will be strong. He does it to get a crown that will soon be worth nothing, but we work for a crown that will last forever.

1 Corinthians 9:24–25

Father God, please remind me every day that I'm in an important race here on earth. You're the best coach I could ever have. Please help me to run well, looking ahead to a perfect forever prize in heaven and enjoying the running and the good plans You have for me along the way. Amen.

DAY 102

Zaccheus, Come Down

[Zaccheus] ran ahead and got up into a sycamore tree to see Him. Jesus was going by that way. When Jesus came to the place, He looked up and saw Zaccheus. He said, "Zaccheus, come down at once. I must stay in your house today." At once he came down and was glad to have Jesus come to his house. When the people saw it, they began to complain. . . . "He is going to stay with a man who is known to be a sinner." Zaccheus stood up and said to the Lord, "Lord, see! Half of what I own I will give to poor people. And if I have taken money from anyone in a wrong way, I will pay him back four times as much." Jesus said to him, "Today, a person has been saved in this house. This man is a Jew also. For the Son of Man came to look for and to save from the punishment of sin those who are lost."

LUKE 19:4–10

Dear Jesus, You didn't reject Zaccheus; You helped him turn away from his sin. Thank You for looking for people to save and rescuing them from the punishment of sin. Amen.

DAY 103

Like Children

At that time the followers came to Jesus. They said, "Who is the greatest in the holy nation of heaven?" Jesus took a little child and put him among them. He said, "For sure, I tell you, unless you have a change of heart and become like a little child, you will not get into the holy nation of heaven. Whoever is without pride as this little child is the greatest in the holy nation of heaven. Whoever receives a little child because of Me receives Me. But whoever is the reason for one of these little children who believe in Me to fall into sin, it would be better for him to have a large rock put around his neck and to be thrown into the sea."

MATTHEW 18:1–6

Dear Jesus, thank You for the way You loved and still love and treasure and protect children like me! Amen.

DAY 104

The Holy Spirit Wouldn't Let Them

They went through the countries of Phrygia and Galatia. The Holy Spirit kept them from preaching the Word of God in the countries of Asia. When they came to the city of Mysia, they tried to go on to the city of Bithynia but the Holy Spirit would not let them go.

Acts 16:6–7

Dear Lord, through Your Holy Spirit, You led Paul and Timothy as they served You. And sometimes Your Spirit stopped them from doing certain things and going certain places. Please do the same for me. Please guide me where You want me to go, and please stop me from going where You don't want me to go. Thank You for leading me with love! Amen.

DAY 105

Learn from Jonah

The Word of the Lord came to Jonah the son of Amittai, saying, "Get up and go to the large city of Nineveh, and preach against it. For their sin has come up before Me." But Jonah ran away from the Lord going toward Tarshish. He went down to Joppa and found a ship which was going to Tarshish. Jonah paid money, and got on the ship to go with them, to get away from the Lord.

JONAH 1:1–3

Dear Father God, help me to learn from Jonah's story. When he disobeyed You and tried to get away from You, he ended up in the belly of a huge fish. Yikes! I want to remember that choosing to disobey You might land me in some really bad situations. When I do obey, I know You are happy and want to bless me with good things—not stinky fish bellies! Amen.

DAY 106

The Vine

"I am the true Vine. My Father is the One Who cares for the Vine. He takes away any branch in Me that does not give fruit. Any branch that gives fruit, He cuts it back so it will give more fruit. You are made clean by the words I have spoken to you. Get your life from Me and I will live in you. No branch can give fruit by itself. It has to get life from the vine. You are able to give fruit only when you have life from Me. I am the Vine and you are the branches. Get your life from Me. Then I will live in you and you will give much fruit. You can do nothing without Me."

John 15:1–5

Dear Jesus, remind me that You are the vine and I am a branch. I cannot truly live without being connected to You. I produce good fruit through my good works when I'm connected to You and getting my life from You. I can do nothing without You. Amen.

DAY 107

Thomas Didn't Believe

Thomas was not with them when Jesus came. He was one of the twelve followers and was called the Twin. The other followers told him, "We have seen the Lord!" He said to them, "I will not believe until I see the marks made by the nails in His hands. I will not believe until I put my finger into the marks of the nails. I will not believe until I put my hand into His side." Eight days later the followers were again inside a house. Thomas was with them. The doors were locked. Jesus came and stood among them. He said, "May you have peace!" He said to Thomas, "Put your finger into My hands. Put your hand into My side. Do not doubt, believe!" Thomas said to Him, "My Lord and my God!" Jesus said to him, "Thomas, because you have seen Me, you believe. Those are happy who have never seen Me and yet believe!"

JOHN 20:24–29

Dear Jesus, help me to remember that those of us who have never seen You in person yet still believe are very happy. We are extra blessed by having faith even without seeing. Please help my faith to keep getting stronger every day. Amen.

DAY 108

Get God's Favor

Do you think I am trying to get the favor of men, or of God? If I were still trying to please men, I would not be a servant owned by Christ.

GALATIANS 1:10

Dear Father God, please help me to want Your favor, not the favor of other people. I want to live to make You happy with me and not just to please other people. If I'm living to make You happy, You will bless me in the perfect ways You want to, and You will bring the right people who love me into my life. If I try to please people instead of You, then I'm not really a servant and follower of Jesus. And nothing in this life is better than being a servant and follower of Jesus. Amen.

DAY 109

Call Out with Joy

Call out with joy to the Lord, all the earth.
Be glad as you serve the Lord. Come before
Him with songs of joy. Know that the Lord is God.
It is He Who made us, and not we ourselves.
We are His people and the sheep of His field.
Go into His gates giving thanks and into His holy
place with praise. Give thanks to Him. Honor His
name. For the Lord is good. His loving-kindness
lasts forever. And He is faithful to all people
and to all their children-to-come.

Psalm 100

Dear Lord, the whole earth should call out with joy and praise to You! I'm so glad I get to know You and serve You. You made every person and every good thing. Your Word says every perfect gift comes from You. You are faithful to all people—past, present, and future. I honor Your name because You are good and loving and kind forever. Amen.

DAY 110

They Kept Teaching and Preaching

They called the missionaries in and beat them. They told them they must not speak in the name of Jesus. Then they were sent away. So the missionaries went away from the court happy that they could suffer shame because of His Name. Every day in the house of God and in the homes, they kept teaching and preaching about Jesus Christ.

ACTS 5:40–42

Wow, Jesus, even when Your followers were beaten and told not to speak of You anymore, they were still happy and they still kept teaching and preaching about You. I want to be as bold and brave as they were—totally unafraid to continue sharing the good news about You! Amen.

DAY 111

Let the Greatest Be as the Least

They started to argue among themselves about who was thought to be the greatest. Jesus said to them, "The kings of the nations show their power to the people. Those who have power over the people are given names of honor. But you will not be like that. Let the greatest among you be as the least. Let the leader be as the one who cares for others. Who is greater, the one who is eating at the table, or the one who is caring for him? Is it not the one who is eating at the table? But I am here with you as One Who cares for you."

LUKE 22:24–27

Dear Jesus, help me not to try to be the greatest. Help me just to be who You want me to be and to serve and care for others well like You do. Amen.

DAY 112

Built on Rock

"Whoever hears these words of Mine and does them, will be like a wise man who built his house on rock. The rain came down. The water came up. The wind blew and hit the house. The house did not fall because it was built on rock. Whoever hears these words of Mine and does not do them, will be like a foolish man who built his house on sand. The rain came down. The water came up. The wind blew and hit the house. The house fell and broke apart."

MATTHEW 7:24–27

Dear Jesus, if I only hear Your Word but don't listen to and obey it, my life will fall apart like sand. I want to be wise. I want to obey You. My life won't fall apart if it's built on You and Your Word. That will make me rock solid. I will be able to stand strong no matter what storms life sends my way. Amen.

DAY 113

Don't Give Up

We are happy for the hope we have of sharing the shining-greatness of God. We are glad for our troubles also. We know that troubles help us learn not to give up. When we have learned not to give up, it shows we have stood the test. When we have stood the test, it gives us hope. Hope never makes us ashamed because the love of God has come into our hearts through the Holy Spirit Who was given to us.

Romans 5:2–5

Father God, I like fun and happy times. I don't like to go through troubles and hard times. Who does? But Your Word tells me to be happy for troubles because of what I can learn from them. When I stay strong in my faith in You during troubles, I can learn not to give up. I can learn to have greater hope. And I can experience more and more of Your love and power in my life through the Holy Spirit. Please remind me of the hidden benefits of going through troubles, and help me to get through them with grace. Amen.

DAY 114

The Lord's Throne Is in Heaven

The Lord is in His holy house. The Lord's throne is in heaven. His eyes see as He tests the sons of men. The Lord tests and proves those who are right and good and those who are sinful. And His soul hates the one who loves to hurt others. He will send down fire upon the sinful. Fire and sulphur and burning wind will be the cup they will drink. For the Lord is right and good. He loves what is right and good. And those who are right with Him will see His face.

PSALM 11:4–7

Dear Lord, I believe You are on Your throne in heaven ruling over all. You are the one true King! You see everything going on in all the world, and You judge who is evil and who is good. You will punish all those who love to hurt others. You are right and good, and You will bring real justice like only You can. Amen.

DAY 115

Two Blind Men

As they went away from the city of Jericho, many people followed Him. Two blind men were sitting by the side of the road. They called out when they heard that Jesus was going by. They said, "Lord, take pity on us, Son of David!" Many people spoke sharp words to them. They told the blind men not to call out. But they called all the more, "Lord! Take pity on us, Son of David!" Jesus stopped and called them. He asked, "What do you want Me to do for you?" The blind men said to Jesus, "Lord, we want our eyes opened!" Jesus had loving-pity on them and put His hands on their eyes. At once they could see, and they followed Jesus.

MATTHEW 20:29–34

Dear Jesus, while others tried to stop the blind men from calling to You for help, You called back to them and then went to them and touched them and healed them. Thank You for Your example of love and compassion. Thank You that I can call on You too and know that You have love and compassion for me. Amen.

DAY 116

Peter's Big Mistake

They built a fire in the yard and sat down. Peter sat down with them. One of the servant-girls saw Peter as he sat by the fire and looked right at him. She said, "This man was with Jesus also." Peter lied and said, "Woman, I do not know Him." After awhile another person saw him and said, "You are one of them also." Peter said, "No, sir, I am not." About an hour later another person said the same thing, "For sure, this man was with Jesus also because he is from Galilee." But Peter said, "Sir, I do not know what you are saying." And at once, while he was talking, a rooster crowed. The Lord turned and looked at Peter. He remembered the Lord had said, "Before a rooster crows, you will say three times that you do not know Me." Peter went outside and cried with a troubled heart.

Luke 22:55–62

Dear Jesus, please help me to learn from Peter's big mistake. I never want to deny that I know and love You as my one and only Savior! I want the world to know that I love and follow You! Amen.

DAY 117

So You Can Always Give to Others

God will give you enough so you can always give to others. Then many will give thanks to God for sending gifts through us. This gift you give not only helps Christians who are in need, but it also helps them give thanks to God. You are proving by this act of love what you are. They will give thanks to God for your gift to them and to others. This proves you obey the Good News of Christ. They will pray for you with great love because God has given you His loving-favor. Thank God for His great Gift.

2 Corinthians 9:11–15

Father God, I want to be the kind of giver You want me to be. Help me now when I'm young to develop a great big love for giving so that I will love to share and be generous all my life. I trust You will always give me enough so that I can always be giving to others. Amen.

DAY 118

Warnings about Riches

Jesus said to His followers, "For sure, I tell you, it will be hard for a rich man to get into the holy nation of heaven. Again I tell you, it is easier for a camel to go through the eye of a needle than for a rich man to get into the holy nation of heaven." When His followers heard this, they could not understand it. They said, "Then who can be saved from the punishment of sin?" Jesus looked at them and said, "This cannot be done by men. But with God all things can be done."

MATTHEW 19:23–26

Dear Jesus, please help me never to put my hopes in money and riches. Your Word warns against loving money. Help me to love and follow You most of all and trust that You will always have just what I need. Amen.

DAY 119

The Story of Tabitha

A woman who was a follower lived in the city of Joppa. Her name was Tabitha, or Dorcas. She did many good things and many acts of kindness. One day she became sick and died. . . . The followers heard that Peter was at Lydda and sent two men to ask him to come at once. Peter went back with them. When he came, they took him to the room. All the women whose husbands had died were standing around crying. They were showing the clothes Dorcas had made while she was with them. Peter made them all leave the room. Then he got down on his knees and prayed. He turned to her body and said, "Tabitha, get up!" She opened her eyes and looked at Peter and sat up. He took her by the hand and lifted her up. Then he called in the faithful followers and the women whose husbands had died. He gave her to them, a living person. News of this went through all Joppa. Many people put their trust in the Lord.

Acts 9:36–42

Dear Lord, when You work miracles, many people put their trust in You! I pray You will keep showing people many miracles! Amen.

DAY 120

The Story of Saul

So Ananias went to that house. He put his hands on Saul and said, "Brother Saul, the Lord Jesus has sent me to you. You saw the Lord along the road as you came here. The Lord has sent me so you might be able to see again and be filled with the Holy Spirit." At once something like a covering fell from the eyes of Saul and he could see. He got up and was baptized. After that he ate some food and received strength. For some days he stayed with the followers in Damascus. At once Saul began to preach in the Jewish places of worship that Jesus is the Son of God. All who heard him were surprised and wondered. They said, "This is the man who beat and killed the followers in Jerusalem. He came here to tie the followers in chains and take them to the head religious leaders." But Saul kept on growing in power.

ACTS 9:17–22

Dear Jesus, help me to remember from the story of Saul that You can completely change someone's life! I pray for the people I know who need a big transformation like only You can bring about. Amen.

DAY 121

So Much Faith

Jesus came to the city of Capernaum. A captain of the army came to Him. He asked for help, saying, "Lord, my servant is sick in bed. He is not able to move his body. He is in much pain." Jesus said to the captain, "I will come and heal him." The captain said, "Lord, I am not good enough for You to come to my house. Only speak the word, and my servant will be healed. I am a man who works for someone else and I have men working under me. I say to this man, 'Go!' and he goes. I say to another, 'Come!' and he comes. I say to my servant, 'Do this!' and he does it." When Jesus heard this, He was surprised and wondered about it. He said to those who followed Him, "For sure, I tell you, I have not found so much faith in the Jewish nation."

MATTHEW 8:5–10

Dear Jesus, please help me to have the same kind of faith this army captain did. I believe You can just say the word and any miracle can happen. You are amazing! Amen.

DAY 122

How Long, Lord?

How long, O Lord? Will You forget me forever?
How long will You hide Your face from me?
How long must I plan what to do in my soul,
and have sorrow in my heart all the day?
How long will those who hate me rise above me?

Psalm 13:1–2

Dear Lord, like this scripture says, sometimes I do feel like You've completely forgotten me. But then I remember all the ways You've shown Your love and care in the past, and I choose to trust You are watching over me now and forever—even if I'm confused and waiting on You in this moment. I will choose to pray, "I have trusted in Your loving-kindness. My heart will be full of joy because You will save me. I will sing to the Lord, because He has been good to me" (Psalm 13:5–6).

DAY 123

Ask God for Wisdom

If you do not have wisdom, ask God for it. He is always ready to give it to you and will never say you are wrong for asking. You must have faith as you ask Him. You must not doubt. Anyone who doubts is like a wave which is pushed around by the sea. Such a man will get nothing from the Lord. The man who has two ways of thinking changes in everything he does.

JAMES 1:5–8

Father God, I like playing in big, choppy waves, but I don't want to be pushed around like a wave in my thinking. I need strong and steady wisdom from You, and I need to trust in it. Thank You for promising to give me insight and understanding every time I ask. I believe in You and in Your perfect wisdom. I want to follow You with strength and confidence! Amen.

DAY 124

Always in Front

I have placed the Lord always in front of me. Because He is at my right hand, I will not be moved. And so my heart is glad. My soul is full of joy. My body also will rest without fear. For You will not give me over to the grave. And You will not allow Your Holy One to return to dust. You will show me the way of life. Being with You is to be full of joy. In Your right hand there is happiness forever.

Psalm 16:8–11

Dear Lord, I want to place You always right in front of me. I want to follow You, not do my own thing. When I do follow You, my heart and soul are full of joy and peace. You show me how to have the very best kind of life and happiness forever. Amen.

DAY 125

Wind and Waves

Jesus got into a boat. His followers followed Him. At once a bad storm came over the lake. The waves were covering the boat. Jesus was sleeping. His followers went to Him and called, "Help us, Lord, or we will die!" He said to them, "Why are you afraid? You have so little faith!" Then He stood up. He spoke sharp words to the wind and the waves. Then the wind stopped blowing. Then men were surprised and wondered about it. They said, "What kind of a man is He? Even the winds and the waves obey Him."

MATTHEW 8:23–27

Dear Jesus, You can command even the most powerful winds and waves to stop, so surely You can stop the storm going on in my life right now. I'm trusting You for that. Please keep me calm and safe. Amen.

DAY 126

The Earth Is Filled with the Fruit of God's Works

[God] covers Himself with light as with a coat. He spreads out the heavens like a tent. He makes His home on the waters. He makes the clouds His wagon. He rides on the wings of the wind. He makes the winds carry His news. He makes His helpers a burning fire. He set the earth in its place so that it will stay that way forever. . . . He sends rivers into the valleys. They flow between the mountains. They give water to all the animals of the field. The wild donkeys drink until they are no longer thirsty. The birds of the sky nest beside them. They sing among the branches. He waters the mountains from His home above. The earth is filled with the fruit of His works. He makes the grass grow for the cattle, and plants for man to use. So He may bring food from the earth, wine that makes man's heart glad, oil to make his face shine, and food to make his heart strong.

Psalm 104:2–5, 10–15

Dear Father God, You're an amazing designer and Creator! I love to read about Your power and Your creation. You are worthy of all my praise! Amen.

DAY 127

Jesus Prayed for His Followers

"I do not pray for these followers only. I pray for those who will put their trust in Me through the teaching they have heard. May they all be as one, Father, as You are in Me and I am in You. May they belong to Us. Then the world will believe that You sent Me. I gave them the honor You gave Me that they may be one as We are One. I am in them and You are in Me so they may be one and be made perfect. Then the world may know that You sent Me and that You love them as You love Me. Father, I want My followers You gave Me to be with Me where I am. Then they may see My shining-greatness which You gave Me because You loved Me before the world was made."

JOHN 17:20–24

Dear Jesus, thank You for the way You prayed for Your followers—including me today! I pray these things along with You now. I am so loved by You, and I love You too. Amen.

DAY 128

Go and Do the Same

Jesus said, "A man was going down from Jerusalem to the city of Jericho. Robbers came out after him. They took his clothes off and beat him. Then they went away, leaving him almost dead. A religious leader was walking down that road and saw the man. But he went by on the other side. In the same way, a man from the family group of Levi was walking down that road. When he saw the man who was hurt, he came near to him but kept on going on the other side of the road. Then a man from the country of Samaria came by. He went up to the man. As he saw him, he had loving-pity on him. . . . Which of these three do you think was a neighbor to the man who was beaten by the robbers?" The man who knew the Law said, "The one who showed loving-pity on him." Then Jesus said, "Go and do the same."

LUKE 10:30–33, 36–37

Dear Jesus, please help me to be like the good man from Samaria. I want to be willing to help people in need, especially when no one else will. Amen.

DAY 129

Crying Turns to Dancing

Hear, O Lord. And show me loving-kindness.
O Lord, be my Helper. You have turned my crying
into dancing. You have. . .dressed me with joy.
So my soul may sing praise to You, and not be quiet.
O Lord my God, I will give thanks to You forever.
Psalm 30:10–12

Dear Lord, my helper, only You can turn my crying into dancing. You have promised that "those who plant with tears will gather fruit with songs of joy" (Psalm 126:5). I trust You when You say the sadness I'm feeling now won't last forever. You will turn it into something good and happy somehow, even if I don't understand how that is possible. I choose to sing praises to You. I give You thanks and worship You always! Amen.

DAY 130

Jesus Can Do Anything in Any Way

Then Jesus left the cities of Tyre and Sidon. He came back to the Sea of Galilee by way of the land of Decapolis. They took a man to Him who could not hear or speak well. They asked Jesus to put His hand on him. Jesus took him away from the other people. He put His fingers into the man's ears. He spit and put His finger on the man's tongue. Then Jesus looked up to heaven and breathed deep within. He said to the man, "Be opened!" At once his ears were opened. His tongue was made loose and he spoke as other people.

MARK 7:31–35

Dear Jesus, You healed people in all kinds of ways. You can do anything in any way You choose. I don't have to understand You completely; I just know You are good and loving in all Your ways. Amen.

DAY 131

God Will Be with You

But now the Lord Who made you, O Jacob, and He Who made you, O Israel, says, "Do not be afraid. For I have bought you and made you free. I have called you by name. You are Mine! When you pass through the waters, I will be with you. When you pass through the rivers, they will not flow over you. When you walk through the fire, you will not be burned. The fire will not destroy you. For I am the Lord your God, the Holy One of Israel, Who saves you. . . . You are of great worth in My eyes. You are honored and I love you."

Isaiah 43:1–4

Dear Lord, You didn't tell Your people they would never go through anything hard. Instead, You told them You would always be with them in the middle of anything hard. That includes me today, because I am Yours. Thank You for always being with me, in the best of times and the worst of times. I feel loved and honored and treasured by You! Amen.

DAY 132

The Greatest of the Laws

He said, "Teacher, which one is the greatest of the Laws?" Jesus said to him, " 'You must love the Lord your God with all your heart and with all your soul and with all your mind.' This is the first and greatest of the Laws. The second is like it, 'You must love your neighbor as you love yourself.' All the Laws and the writings of the early preachers depend on these two most important Laws."

MATTHEW 22:35–40

Dear Jesus, please help me never to forget the greatest commandment to love God with all my heart and soul and mind. And help me never to forget the second-greatest commandment to love my neighbor as myself. I want to honor and obey You. I want to grow in Your love and share it with others. Amen.

DAY 133

Good Medicine

A glad heart is good medicine,
but a broken spirit dries up the bones.
PROVERBS 17:22

Father God, I don't usually like medicine, but a glad heart doesn't sound bad at all! Help me to remember this scripture. When I focus on Your goodness and love for me, I can be full of joy and have a glad heart in the middle of any hard thing—in any sickness or trouble I'm going through. And that glad heart will help me get well and not give up. Help me not to feel broken and sad and gloomy. I want to smile and laugh a lot every day. Show me all the reasons I have to be thankful and full of joy—especially because You have saved me through Jesus! Amen.

DAY 134

Don't Be Lazy

Do not be lazy but always work hard. Work for the Lord with a heart full of love for Him.

ROMANS 12:11

Dear Lord, I'm sorry. I need to confess the ways I'm really lazy sometimes. I get stuck wanting to just sit on the couch and watch TV or play video games or other silly stuff. I know those things don't have to be wrong if they're not bad and are just fun some of the time. But they become wrong if I let them use up all my time and take me away from the things You want me to do. Help me to love to work hard and do everything with my heart full of love for You. I can do any job or task or chore with a good attitude and gratefulness as a way to worship You and thank You for my abilities. Amen.

DAY 135

God's Ways and Paths

Show me Your ways, O Lord. Teach me Your paths. Lead me in Your truth and teach me. For You are the God Who saves me. I wait for You all day long. Remember Your loving-pity and Your loving-kindness, O Lord. For they have been from old. Do not remember my sins from when I was young, or my sinful ways. By Your loving-kindness remember me for You are good, O Lord.

Psalm 25:4–7

Dear Lord, I pray this psalm to You. I do want to know Your ways and paths because I believe they are the best for me. Lead me and guide me, for You are the one true God who saves me. Forgive and forget my sins like only You can, Father. Thank You for being so loving and so good! Amen.

DAY 136

Watch and Pray

"Be careful! Watch and pray. You do not know when it will happen. The coming of the Son of Man is as a man who went from his house to a far country. He gave each one of his servants some work to do. He told the one standing at the door to watch. In the same way, you are to watch also! You do not know when the Owner of the house will be coming. It may be in the evening or in the night or when the sun comes up or in the morning. He may come when you are not looking for Him and find you sleeping. What I say to you, I say to all. Watch!"

MARK 13:33–37

Dear Jesus, You could come back at any time; no one knows exactly when You'll return. Help me to be watching and praying as I wait for that day. I'll keep on living my life for You until You come. Until then, show me all the good things You want me to do! Amen.

DAY 137

Jesus Healed Them

Jesus went from there and came to the Sea of Galilee. Then He went up the mountain and sat down. Many people came to Him. They brought with them those who were not able to walk. They brought those who were not able to see. They brought those who were not able to hear or speak and many others. Then they put them at the feet of Jesus and He healed them. All the people wondered. They saw how those who could not speak were now talking. They saw how those who could not walk were now walking. They saw how those who could not see were now seeing, and they gave thanks to the God of the Jews.

MATTHEW 15:29–31

Dear Jesus, watching You heal people from all kinds of sicknesses and suffering must have been amazing. I know Your healing power is still on earth today through the Holy Spirit. I pray for those I know who are sick and suffering. Please heal them in miraculous ways, Lord. Amen.

DAY 138

Eyes on the Lord

Who is the man who fears the Lord? He will teach him in the way he should choose. His soul will live a rich life. And his children will be given the land. The secret of the Lord is for those who fear Him. And He will make them know His agreement. My eyes are always on the Lord.

Psalm 25:12–15

Dear Lord, I fear You—not in a scared kind of way but in a respectful kind of way. You are almighty God! I trust You to teach me and guide me to make good choices. I believe You will give me a rich life, not in a having-lots-of-money kind of way but in the best kind of way—a life rich with love and peace and purpose. I want to keep my eyes always on You! Amen.

DAY 139

What God Wants

He began to have much sorrow and a heavy heart. He said to them, "My soul is very sad. My soul is so full of sorrow I am ready to die. You stay here and watch." He went a little farther and got down with His face on the ground. He prayed that this time of suffering might pass from Him if it could. He said, "Father, You can do all things. Take away what must happen to Me. Even so, not what I want, but what You want."

MARK 14:33–36

Dear Jesus, You know what feeling sad and anxious is like. You were sad and anxious before the time came for You to be crucified. But even as You prayed for God the Father to take away the bad things that were about to happen to You, You also prayed for what God wanted, not just what You wanted in Your human form. Help me to learn from You. Help me to want the Father's good plans for me most of all. Amen.

DAY 140

Be Holy

Get your minds ready for good use. Keep awake. Set your hope now and forever on the loving-favor to be given you when Jesus Christ comes again. Be like children who obey. Do not desire to sin like you used to when you did not know any better. Be holy in every part of your life. Be like the Holy One Who chose you. The Holy Writings say, "You must be holy, for I am holy."

1 Peter 1:13–16

Dear Father God, please help me to stay away from what is bad and sinful in the things I say and think and do. Help my thoughts to be clean and good and my mind ready to do what You ask me to do. I want to obey You. I need Your grace through Jesus to make me holy, because I can't become holy on my own. I want to be right with You and righteous before You. Amen.

DAY 141

Be True

Put out of your life hate and lying. Do not pretend to be someone you are not. Do not always want something someone else has. Do not say bad things about other people.

1 Peter 2:1

Dear Lord, help me to be true in all that I do. Help me never to pretend to be someone I am not. Help me not to be jealous over things that other people have that I don't. Help me not to say bad things about other people either. Following these good rules for living is hard sometimes, Lord, especially with my friends and classmates. Please forgive me for the times I mess up, and help me to do better moving forward. Amen.

DAY 142

Give

"Give, and it will be given to you. You will have more than enough. It can be pushed down and shaken together and it will still run over as it is given to you. The way you give to others is the way you will receive in return."
LUKE 6:38

Dear Jesus, please help me to love to give. You've promised that if I give, it will be given to me. The way I give is the way I will get back in return. If I give only a little, I will get only a little. But if I love to give a lot, I will get a lot! Help me to be generous and not selfish—with my stuff, with my money, with my time, and with my talents. Amen.

DAY 143

The Father's House

It was time for the special religious gathering to remember how the Jews left Egypt. Jesus went up to Jerusalem. He went into the house of God and found cattle and sheep and doves being sold. Men were sitting there changing money. Jesus made a whip of small ropes. He used it to make them all leave the house of God along with the sheep and cattle. He pushed their money off the tables and turned the tables over. He said to those who sold doves, "Take these things out of here! You must not make My Father's house a place for buying and selling!"

John 2:13–16

Dear Jesus, please help me always to respect the Father's house the way You want me to. It's a special place for worshipping and honoring and serving You. Amen.

DAY 144

Choose the Good Thing

As they went on their way, they came to a town where a woman named Martha lived. She cared for Jesus in her home. Martha had a sister named Mary. Mary sat at the feet of Jesus and listened to all He said. Martha was working hard getting the supper ready. She came to Jesus and said, "Do You see that my sister is not helping me? Tell her to help me." Jesus said to her, "Martha, Martha, you are worried and troubled about many things. Only a few things are important, even just one. Mary has chosen the good thing. It will not be taken away from her."

Luke 10:38–42

Dear Jesus, help me not to be worried and troubled about many things like Martha. Help me to be more like Mary, who simply wanted to sit at Your feet and listen to You. I want to listen closely to You too. Amen.

DAY 145

The Son of the Living God

Jesus said to the twelve followers, "Will you leave Me also?" Simon Peter said to Him, "Lord, who else can we go to? You have words that give life that lasts forever. We believe and know You are the Christ. You are the Son of the Living God."

John 6:67–69

Dear Jesus, I will never turn to anyone else but You! Why would I? No one else has the words that give eternal life. I put my faith in You alone. You are the Christ. You are the Son of the living God! I believe in You with all my heart and mind forever. Amen.

DAY 146

He Is Risen!

Very early in the morning on the first day of the week, they came to the grave. The sun had come up. They said to themselves, "Who will roll the stone away from the door of the grave for us?" But when they looked, they saw the very large stone had been rolled away. They went into the grave. There they saw a young man with a long white coat sitting on the right side. They were afraid. He said, "Do not be afraid. You are looking for Jesus of Nazareth Who was nailed to a cross. He is risen! He is not here!"

MARK 16:2–6

Dear Jesus, You were killed in such a horrible way, and my heart hurts when I think of the pain You endured for my sake. You suffered and died to take the punishment for everyone's sin. But You didn't stay dead! The way You rose again is amazing—I have hope because of You! You give eternal life to all who believe in You as their Savior from sin. I can never thank You enough! Amen.

DAY 147

No Worries

"I tell you this: Do not worry about your life. Do not worry about what you are going to eat and drink. Do not worry about what you are going to wear. Is not life more important than food? Is not the body more important than clothes? Look at the birds in the sky. They do not plant seeds. They do not gather grain. They do not put grain into a building to keep. Yet your Father in heaven feeds them! Are you not more important than the birds?"

Matthew 6:25–26

Dear Jesus, You've told me not to worry about my life, and I want to obey. You will provide everything I truly need. Every time I see a bird in the sky, help me to remember this scripture. You take such good care of the birds, and I'm even more important to You than they are, so I know You'll take good care of me too. Thank You! Amen.

DAY 148

With All Your Heart

Trust in the Lord with all your heart, and do not trust in your own understanding. Agree with Him in all your ways, and He will make your paths straight. Do not be wise in your own eyes. Fear the Lord and turn away from what is sinful. It will be healing to your body and medicine to your bones.

PROVERBS 3:5–8

Dear Lord, I want to trust in You with all my heart. My own thinking is sometimes wrong and confused. Please replace it with Your thoughts and wisdom and understanding. Please make my hopes and dreams match what You have planned for me. Help me to turn away from sinful things and look to You always. Amen.

DAY 149

Honor and Thanks

May honor and thanks be given to the Lord, because He has heard my prayer. The Lord is my strength and my safe cover. My heart trusts in Him, and I am helped. So my heart is full of joy. I will thank Him with my song. The Lord is the strength of His people. He is a safe place for His chosen one. Save Your people and bring good to what is Yours. Be their shepherd and carry them forever.

PSALM 28:6–9

Dear Lord, You give me help when I trust in You. You are my strength and joy. You are my Shepherd. You love me and carry me and bring good things to me. I sing praises to You, Lord! I give all honor and thanks to You! Amen.

DAY 150

Lord, Teach Us to Pray

Jesus had been praying. One of His followers said to Him, "Lord, teach us to pray as John the Baptist taught his followers." Jesus said to them, "When you pray, say, 'Our Father in heaven, Your name is holy. May Your holy nation come. What You want done, may it be done on earth as it is in heaven. Give us the bread we need everyday. Forgive us our sins, as we forgive those who sin against us. Do not let us be tempted.'"

LUKE 11:1–4

Dear Jesus, I know I can pray to You about anything and everything, but I'm thankful for the example You gave. I want to worship You. I want Your will to be done. I ask You to supply what I need and to forgive my sins. Help me to forgive others, and help me not to be tempted. Thank You for teaching us to pray! Amen.

DAY 151

More Than Enough

Each man should give as he has decided in his heart. He should not give, wishing he could keep it. Or he should not give if he feels he has to give. God loves a man who gives because he wants to give. God can give you all you need. He will give you more than enough. You will have everything you need for yourselves. And you will have enough left over to give when there is a need.

2 Corinthians 9:7–8

Dear Lord, please help me to be a cheerful giver. Help me to love sharing my stuff, my money, my time, and my talents. All those things are gifts from You anyway, and I want to delight in sharing them with others. I trust that when I give, You will always be showering me with more blessings so I can continue to share. Thank You! Amen.

DAY 152

Strangers Here

Dear friends, your real home is not here on earth. You are strangers here. I ask you to keep away from all the sinful desires of the flesh. These things fight to get hold of your soul. When you are around people who do not know God, be careful how you act. Even if they talk against you as wrong-doers, in the end they will give thanks to God for your good works when Christ comes again.

1 Peter 2:11–12

Father God, thank You for my home here on earth, but help me to remember it's not my real home. This home is just for a little while. My home in heaven is forever. I feel like a stranger here on this earth as I try my best to follow Your ways and obey Your Word. Please help me to keep on following You no matter what and to stay away from sinful things. Amen.

DAY 153

The Voice of the Lord

The voice of the Lord is powerful. The voice of the Lord is great. The voice of the Lord breaks the cedars. . . . The voice of the Lord sends out lightning. The voice of the Lord shakes the desert. The Lord shakes the desert of Kadesh. The voice of the Lord makes the deer give birth, and tears away the leaves of the trees. And in His holy house everything says, "Honor to God!"

PSALM 29:4–5, 7–9

Dear Lord, with just Your voice, You can do anything at all! Your voice is powerful beyond all my imagination. I can be strong and brave because I am protected by You and Your voice, almighty God! I honor and praise You! Amen.

DAY 154

Comfort and More Comfort

We give thanks to the God and Father of our Lord Jesus Christ. He is our Father Who shows us loving-kindness and our God Who gives us comfort. He gives us comfort in all our troubles. Then we can comfort other people who have the same troubles. We give the same kind of comfort God gives us.

2 CORINTHIANS 1:3–4

Dear Father God, thank You for all the ways You comfort me when I'm going through troubles. You've especially used the people who love me to help me. Now I want to remember all those ways and share that same kind of comfort with others as they go through troubles. What a blessing to be able to keep passing Your comfort on and on and on! Amen.

DAY 155

You Were Chosen

You were chosen by God the Father long ago. He knew you were to become His children. You were set apart for holy living by the Holy Spirit. May you obey Jesus Christ and be made clean by His blood. May you be full of His loving-favor and peace.

1 Peter 1:2

Dear Lord, I'm astounded when I think of how I was chosen by You long ago—before I was even born. You knew I would become Your child. You set me apart for holy living through the help of the Holy Spirit. The blood Jesus shed when He died on the cross for me has washed away all my sin, and now I want to serve You all my life. I could never say thank You enough for Your love and kindness! Amen.

DAY 156

An Eight-Year-Old King

Josiah was eight years old when he became king. He ruled for thirty-one years in Jerusalem. His mother's name was Jedidah the daughter of Adaiah of Bozkath. Josiah did what is right in the eyes of the Lord. He walked in all the way of his father David. He did not turn aside to the right or to the left.

2 Kings 22:1–2

Wow, Lord—Josiah was just a kid like me when he became king! I'm not sure I'll ever be a royal ruler, but I want to be described like Josiah anyway. I always want to do what is right in Your eyes. I want to walk in the ways of the good role models in my life—the ones who love and obey You. I never want to turn aside from following You! I need Your help to walk in Your ways, and I trust You to keep giving it. Thank You! Amen.

DAY 157

Stand Strong

Keep awake! Watch at all times. The devil is working against you. He is walking around like a hungry lion with his mouth open. He is looking for someone to eat. Stand against him and be strong in your faith.

1 Peter 5:8–9

Father God, please help me not to be lazy or careless. I constantly need to watch out for the ways the devil is working against me. He wants me to sin and he wants to eat me up like a lion would. He can tear me apart if I don't stand strong against him. So I will stand strong in my faith in You, Lord God! You are always greater within me than anything the devil can try to do to me. Help me to see and stop his evil plans to harm me and my relationship with You. Amen.

DAY 158

Check Your Eyes

"Why do you look at the small piece of wood in your brother's eye and do not see the big piece of wood in your own eye? How can you say to your brother, 'Let me take that small piece of wood out of your eye,' when you do not see the big piece of wood in your own eye? You pretend to be someone you are not. First, take the big piece of wood out of your own eye. Then you can see better to take the small piece of wood out of your brother's eye."

LUKE 6:41–42

Dear Jesus, I've learned that this scripture is about judging others' sin before I notice my own sin. I shouldn't do that! Before I get upset about someone else's mistakes and problems, I should be sure I'm correcting my own mistakes and problems. Then I can help other people better. Please help me to keep learning more about dealing with my own issues first. Amen.

DAY 159

The Light of the World

Jesus spoke to all the people, saying,
"I am the Light of the world. Anyone
who follows Me will not walk in darkness.
He will have the Light of Life."
John 8:12

Dear Jesus, I'm so grateful You are the light of the world. The world today seems very dark in many ways. So many bad things happen, and so many people do bad things. But no one has to walk in darkness if they just follow You! You shine bright against the darkness. I can shine bright against it too because You're living within me and giving me the light of life through Your Holy Spirit. You give people hope, and I can give people hope too as I point them to You! Amen.

DAY 160

Do Not Fear

"Do not fear, for I am with you. Do not be afraid, for I am your God. I will give you strength, and for sure I will help you. Yes, I will hold you up with My right hand that is right and good."

ISAIAH 41:10

Father God, Your Word says, "Do not fear," but I'm still feeling afraid. Please make these fearful thoughts go away. The world is scary sometimes; school troubles are scary sometimes; family troubles are scary sometimes. . . . You know the exact trouble I'm going through right now. But I can't forget that You are with me. You are my God, and You promise to give me strength and help me. Let me feel Your hand holding me up and leading me. You are good, Lord, and I trust You! Amen.

DAY 161

God's Family

The mother of Jesus and His brothers came to Him. They could not get near Him because of so many people. Someone said to Jesus, "Your mother and brothers are standing outside. They want to see You." Jesus said to them, "My mother and brothers are these who hear the Word of God and do it."

LUKE 8:19–21

Dear Jesus, thank You for all the family members You've given me. All those who love You and follow Your Word are my family too. Help us to be grateful for each other, to love each other well, and to take good care of each other. Help us to have a lot of fun too as we worship and serve You together. Amen.

DAY 162

More and More

This faith comes from our God and Jesus Christ, the One Who saves. May you have more and more of His loving-favor and peace as you come to know God and our Lord Jesus Christ better.

2 Peter 1:1–2

Dear Jesus, I'm so grateful for my faith in You! It is such a precious gift. I don't know how anyone lives without You in their life! Please help me to share Your love and truth with others so that they can know You and be saved. And help me to keep experiencing more and more of Your love and blessings and peace in my life as I get to know You better and better every day! Please grow my faith in You big and strong so that nothing can shake it. Amen.

DAY 163

God Gives and Takes Away

"The Lord gave and the Lord has taken away. Praise the name of the Lord." In all this Job did not sin or blame God.

Job 1:21–22

Dear Lord, I've heard about the man named Job in the Bible who went through really hard times. Almost everything he had and everyone he loved was taken away from him. What a horrible experience. Yet I want to remember what he said in this scripture. Job knew that everything comes from You and that You give and take away. Even when You take away, You still deserve worship and praise because You are so good. You are working for my good even in the hard times, and You will always take care of me and give me what I need. What's more, I have forever in heaven to look forward to! Thank You! Amen.

DAY 164

When the Helper Comes

"When the Helper comes, He will show the world the truth about sin. He will show the world about being right with God. And He will show the world what it is to be guilty. He will show the world about sin, because they do not put their trust in Me. He will show the world about being right with God, because I go to My Father and you will see Me no more. He will show the world what it is to be guilty because the leader of this world (Satan) is guilty."

JOHN 16:8–11

Dear Jesus, thank You for sending the Helper, the Holy Spirit, to show the world about sin and about being right with God. We can only be right with God the Father through You, because You took the punishment for sin when You died on the cross. I'm so thankful You rose to life again and are my Savior. Amen.

DAY 165

Have True Love

Most of all, have a true love for each other. Love covers many sins.

1 Peter 4:8

Dear Father God, thank You for this scripture. Especially with my family, I need to remember it well. I fight with my siblings, and I disobey my parents and have a bad attitude sometimes. Thank You that our love for each other can help cover many sins. Help us to say we're sorry and ask for forgiveness and then forgive each other. Help us to tell each other and show each other every day how much we love each other. I'm grateful for my family, Lord. Thank You for giving them to me. Help us to be a family that always wants to trust and honor You. Amen.

DAY 166

Loaves and Fish

When it was evening, His followers came to Him. They said, "This is a desert. The day is past. Send the people away so they may go into the towns and buy food for themselves." Jesus said to them, "They do not have to go away. Give them something to eat." They said to Him, "We have only five loaves of bread and two fish." Jesus said, "Bring them to Me." He told the people to sit down on the grass. Then He took the five loaves of bread and two fish. He looked up to heaven and gave thanks. He broke the loaves in pieces and gave them to His followers. The followers gave them to the people. They all ate and were filled. They picked up twelve baskets full of pieces of bread and fish after the people were finished eating. About five thousand men ate. Women and children ate also.

MATTHEW 14:15–21

Dear Jesus, You took a small lunch and turned it into a feast for thousands of people. And there were even leftovers! You can provide anything and do any kind of miracle. You are awesome, Lord! Amen.

DAY 167

The Good Shepherd

"I am the Good Shepherd. The Good Shepherd gives His life for the sheep. One who is hired to watch the sheep is not the shepherd. He does not own the sheep. He sees the wolf coming and leaves the sheep. He runs away while the wolf gets the sheep and makes them run everywhere. The hired man runs away because he is hired. He does not care about the sheep. I am the Good Shepherd. I know My sheep and My sheep know Me. I know My Father as My Father knows Me. I give My life for the sheep."

JOHN 10:11–15

Dear Jesus, thank You for being my Good Shepherd. Thank You that You know me and I know You. I feel so loved and protected and cared for. You gave Your life for me, and You give me hope and peace and eternal life. I can never thank You enough! Amen.

DAY 168

Who Is Jesus?

While Jesus was praying alone, His followers were with Him. Jesus asked them, "Who do people say that I am?" They said, "John the Baptist, but some say Elijah. Others say that one of the early preachers has been raised from the dead." Jesus said to them, "But who do you say that I am?" Peter said, "You are the Christ of God."

Luke 9:18–20

Dear Jesus, just like Peter declared, I also say that You are the Christ of God! I know who You are—You are my God and my Savior, my Redeemer and my friend! You are the way, truth, and life. I'm so grateful to belong to You. Thank You! Amen.

DAY 169

Seeds in the Ground

"Listen to the picture-story of the man who planted seeds in the ground. When anyone hears the Word about the holy nation and does not understand it, the devil comes and takes away what was put in his heart. He is like the seed that fell by the side of the road. The seed which fell between rocks is like the person who receives the Word with joy as soon as he hears it. Its root is not deep and it does not last long. When troubles and suffering come because of the Word, he gives up and falls away. The seed which fell among thorns is like the person who hears the Word but the cares of this life, and the love for money let the thorns come up and do not give the seed room to grow and give grain. The seed which fell on good ground is like the one who hears the Word and understands it. He gives much grain."

MATTHEW 13:18–23

Dear Jesus, I want to be like the seeds that fell on good ground. I want to hear, understand, and obey Your Word all my life. Amen.

DAY 170

Keep Yourself in the Love of God

You must become strong in your most holy faith. Let the Holy Spirit lead you as you pray. Keep yourselves in the love of God. Wait for life that lasts forever through the loving-kindness of our Lord Jesus Christ.

JUDE 1:20–21

Dear Lord, please make me stronger and stronger in my faith in You. I want to keep myself in Your love every day. Let the Holy Spirit lead me in my prayers. Bring to mind what You want me to be praying about—for others and for myself. Help me to wait for You patiently. I know You give life that lasts forever! Amen.

DAY 171

Priceless Promises

He gives us everything we need for life and for holy living. He gives it through His great power. As we come to know Him better, we learn that He called us to share His own shining-greatness and perfect life. Through His shining-greatness and perfect life, He has given us promises. These promises are of great worth and no amount of money can buy them. Through these promises you can have God's own life in you now that you have gotten away from the sinful things of the world which came from wrong desires of the flesh.

2 Peter 1:3–4

Dear Jesus, thank You for giving me everything I need. Every promise in Your Word is true, and I can believe in and stand on these promises so that I can live the best kind of life, the life You created me for. Amen.

DAY 172

Christ Makes You Complete

Be careful that no one changes your mind and faith by much learning and big sounding ideas. Those things are what men dream up. They are always trying to make new religions. These leave out Christ. For Christ is not only God-like, He is God in human flesh. When you have Christ, you are complete. He is the head over all leaders and powers. When you became a Christian, you were set free from the sinful things of the world.

COLOSSIANS 2:8–11

You are everything, Jesus! I am complete because I have You as my Savior. You set me free from all the sinful, bad things of this world. Please help me never to let anyone change my mind about loving and following You. Amen.

DAY 173

Praise!

Praise the Lord! Praise God in His holy place! Praise Him in the heavens of His power! Praise Him for His great works! Praise Him for all His greatness! Praise Him with the sound of a horn. Praise Him with harps. Praise Him with timbrels and dancing. Praise Him with strings and horns. Praise Him with loud sounds. Praise Him with loud and clear sounds. Let everything that has breath praise the Lord. Praise the Lord!

PSALM 150

Dear Lord, I see a theme in this psalm. I sure am called to praise You. And giving You praise brings so much blessing. When I worship You, I forget any troubles I'm going through. When I focus on Your power and Your greatness and Your love, I have nothing to fear. With everything I am and everything I have, I want to praise You all the time! Amen.

DAY 174

God So Loved

"God so loved the world that He gave His only Son. Whoever puts his trust in God's Son will not be lost but will have life that lasts forever. For God did not send His Son into the world to say it is guilty. He sent His Son so the world might be saved from the punishment of sin by Him. Whoever puts his trust in His Son is not guilty. Whoever does not put his trust in Him is guilty already. It is because he does not put his trust in the name of the only Son of God."

JOHN 3:16–18

Father God, You offer real hope and salvation to everyone everywhere, no matter who they are or what they've done. You so loved the world that You gave Your only Son, that whoever believes in Him should not be lost but have eternal life. I'm so glad I know You as my Savior. Please help me to share Your love so others can know You as Savior too. Amen.

DAY 175

The Gear God Gives You

Put on all the things God gives you to fight with. Then you will be able to stand in that sinful day. When it is all over, you will still be standing. So stand up and do not be moved. Wear a belt of truth around your body. Wear a piece of iron over your chest which is being right with God. Wear shoes on your feet which are the Good News of peace. Most important of all, you need a covering of faith in front of you. This is to put out the fire-arrows of the devil. The covering for your head is that you have been saved from the punishment of sin. Take the sword of the Spirit which is the Word of God.

Ephesians 6:13–17

Dear Lord, You've given me some awesome gear to be able to fight the evil things that come at me in this world. Thank You for equipping me and protecting me! Amen.

DAY 176

No Doubt

Abraham did not doubt God's promise. His faith in God was strong, and he gave thanks to God. He was sure God was able to do what He had promised. Abraham put his trust in God and was made right with Him. The words, "He was made right with God," were not for Abraham only. They were for us also. God will make us right with Himself the same way He did Abraham, if we put our trust in God Who raised Jesus our Lord from the dead. Jesus died for our sins. He was raised from the dead to make us right with God.

ROMANS 4:20–25

Dear Father God, just like Abraham, I don't want to doubt You. I want my faith to be strong. I believe You are able to do what You've promised. I know I am right with You because You sent Your Son, Jesus, to die for my sin, and I trust in the work He did on the cross. Then He rose from the dead so that all who believe in Him can spend eternity with You! This is the absolute best gift ever! Thank You, thank You, thank You! Amen.

DAY 177

Sleep in Peace

I will lie down and sleep in peace.
O Lord, You alone keep me safe.
Psalm 4:8

Dear Lord, sometimes I feel afraid at night. I hear about scary things, and then when I'm lying in my bed in the dark, I think about those scary things. I have a good imagination, and sometimes it runs totally wild. Please help me when I'm scared. Remind me of this scripture every night. I can lie down and sleep in peace because You alone keep me safe. Nothing can harm me when You're watching over me. Nothing is bigger or more powerful than You, not even my imagination. Amen.

DAY 178

Because They Had Faith

What more should I say? There is not enough time to tell of Gideon and of Barak and of Samson and of Jephthah and of David and of Samuel and of the early preachers. It was because these people had faith that they won wars over other countries. They were good leaders. They received what God promised to them. They closed the mouths of lions and stopped fire that was burning. They got away from being killed with swords. They were made strong again after they had been weak and sick. They were strong in war. They made fighting men from other countries run home.

Hebrews 11:32–34

Father God, help me to learn from the stories of faith of people like Gideon, Barak, Samson, Jephthah, David, Samuel, and all the prophets. They were able to do amazing things because they believed in You and Your Holy Spirit was working through them. I want to be like them. Amen.

DAY 179

The Lord Is Your Helper

Keep your lives free from the love of money.
Be happy with what you have. God has said,
"I will never leave you or let you be alone."
So we can say for sure, "The Lord is my Helper.
I am not afraid of anything man can do to me."

HEBREWS 13:5–6

Dear Lord, help me to be content and courageous. You have promised never to leave me or let me be alone. Like this scripture says, I can say for sure that You are my helper, and I'm not afraid of anything anyone can do to me. No person or problem here on this earth is ever more powerful than You. Nothing can defeat me when You are defending me. Help me to always trust in You and stay close to You. Amen.

DAY 180

The Spirit God Gives

God did not give us a spirit of fear. He gave us a spirit of power and of love and of a good mind.

2 Timothy 1:7

Dear Father God, Your Holy Spirit within me is no wimp. You are strong and brave. You are full of love and power! And You make me strong and brave; You fill me with love and power. You give me a good mind that thinks wisely and clearly. Help me not to forget these truths. No matter what I'm facing, I never face it alone because You are within me through Your Holy Spirit. No test or bully or any scary thing can ever defeat me. I have nothing to fear. Amen.

DAY 181

A Hope That Never Dies

Let us thank the God and Father of our Lord Jesus Christ. It was through His loving-kindness that we were born again to a new life and have a hope that never dies. This hope is ours because Jesus was raised from the dead. We will receive the great things that we have been promised. They are being kept safe in heaven for us. They are pure and will not pass away. They will never be lost. You are being kept by the power of God because you put your trust in Him and you will be saved from the punishment of sin at the end of the world.

1 PETER 1:3–5

Dear Lord, I'm so thankful I have hope that never dies because of Jesus! You've given me a life here on earth so I can do the good things You have planned for me, and You're keeping eternal life and awesome blessings in heaven for me to enjoy forever there with You! What amazing gifts! Thank You! Amen.

DAY 182

In God's Hands

But as for me, I trust in You, O Lord. I say, "You are my God." My times are in Your hands.

Psalm 31:14–15

Dear Father God, thank You that my times are in Your hands! I'm picturing a clock with all the hours of my life, and You are holding it and taking care of me every second of every day. Please guide my times and help me to follow. Guide me to the places You want me to be. Guide me to the good things You want me to do with the good gifts You've given me. And guide me to the people You want me to share Your love and truth with. There is no better place for my times to be than in Your hands. Amen.

DAY 183

Wait upon the Lord

They who wait upon the Lord will get new strength. They will rise up with wings like eagles. They will run and not get tired. They will walk and not become weak.

Isaiah 40:31

Dear Lord, I'm tired of this problem that's going on in my life. You know what it is and You know how I'm struggling with it. I'm waiting on You for new strength. Your Word promises You will give it. I can't wait to rise above this problem like an eagle. I can't wait to have fresh energy. Please help me to wait on You patiently and also to sense Your great love for me while I wait. I'm trusting in You, Lord! Amen.

DAY 184

Not Ashamed

I am not ashamed of the Good News. It is the power of God. It is the way He saves men from the punishment of their sins if they put their trust in Him. It is for the Jew first and for all other people also. The Good News tells us we are made right with God by faith in Him. Then, by faith we live that new life through Him. The Holy Writings say, "A man right with God lives by faith."

Romans 1:16–17

Father God, I always want to be able to say like the apostle Paul did that I am not ashamed of the good news of Your saving power. It is the way You save people from sin if they put their trust in Your Son, Jesus. Your good news lets all people know that we are made right with You by faith in Jesus. Thank You so much for Your good news for all people! You are so good and loving, Lord. You are the one true God! Amen.

DAY 185

Wonderful Things

The Holy Writings say, "No eye has ever seen or no ear has ever heard or no mind has ever thought of the wonderful things God has made ready for those who love Him." God has shown these things to us through His Holy Spirit. It is the Holy Spirit Who looks into all things, even the secrets of God, and shows them to us.

1 Corinthians 2:9–10

Father God, I believe You have the most wonderful things planned for everyone who loves You. That includes me! I trust Your Word that says my eyes have never seen anything like the amazing things You are preparing for me. My ears have never heard of anything like them. My mind can't even dream up Your awesome gifts and blessings. Wow! I sure do love You! I'm so grateful I am Yours. Amen.

DAY 186

Say What Is Good

No bad words should be coming from your mouth. Say what is good. Your words should help others grow as Christians. Do not make God's Holy Spirit have sorrow for the way you live. The Holy Spirit has put a mark on you for the day you will be set free. Put out of your life all these things: bad feelings about other people, anger, temper, loud talk, bad talk which hurts other people, and bad feelings which hurt other people. You must be kind to each other.

EPHESIANS 4:29–32

Dear Lord, even just a little encouragement can go a long way! Please help my friends and family and me to share good and kind and positive words with each other. Help us to spur each other on in our faith in You. Help us to get rid of all the bad things in our lives so we can honor You. Amen.

DAY 187

We Will Not Be Afraid

God is our safe place and our strength. He is always our help when we are in trouble. So we will not be afraid, even if the earth is shaken and the mountains fall into the center of the sea, and even if its waters go wild with storm and the mountains shake with its action.

Psalm 46:1–3

Dear Father God, even if the craziest things, like the mountains falling into the center of the sea, are going on around me, I don't need to have any fear. Your Word promises You are my safe place and my strength, and You will always help when I'm in trouble. Whenever I start to feel afraid of anything, please remind me of this scripture and of Your great big power and love. Amen.

DAY 188

Turn from Your Sinful Ways

"Say to them, 'As I live,' says the Lord God, 'I am not pleased when sinful people die. But I am pleased when the sinful turn from their way and live. Turn! Turn from your sinful ways!' "

EZEKIEL 33:11

Father God, I'm so thankful You have such great love for all people. You're not happy when sinful people die. You want them to turn from their sinful ways. You want to save people from sin. That's why You sent Your Son, Jesus, to die on the cross to take the punishment for the sins of everyone in the world. I pray more and more people would believe that good news. Help me to share with others how much You want them to turn from sin and be saved by faith in Jesus. Amen.

DAY 189

Don't Be Troubled

"Do not let your heart be troubled. You have put your trust in God, put your trust in Me also. There are many rooms in My Father's house. If it were not so, I would have told you. I am going away to make a place for you. After I go and make a place for you, I will come back and take you with Me. Then you may be where I am."

JOHN 14:1–3

Dear Jesus, remind me that I never need to be troubled if I've put my trust in You. You are in heaven making a perfect place for me, and someday You will take me there. Meanwhile You help me here and now on earth with anything and everything I need. Thank You! Amen.

DAY 190

But Do Not Be Afraid

"You will hear of wars and lots of talk about wars, but do not be afraid. These things must happen, but it is not the end yet."

MATTHEW 24:6

Dear Jesus, sometimes I hear of scary things on the news like wars and fighting. But You said these things would happen and that I shouldn't be afraid. Please help me to remember that You are in control of everything. You are the beginning and the end of everything. You will win over all evil and scary things someday. Help me to trust in Your perfect timing. In the meantime, help me to do the good things You have planned for me to do, sharing Your love and truth with those around me. Amen.

DAY 191

Not Your Battle

"The Lord says to you, 'Do not be afraid or troubled because of these many men. For the battle is not yours but God's. . . . You will not need to fight in this battle. Just stand still in your places and see the saving power of the Lord work for you, O Judah and Jerusalem.' Do not be afraid or troubled. Go out against them tomorrow, for the Lord is with you."

2 Chronicles 20:15, 17

Dear Father God, when problems in my life seem way too big, help me to remember this story. You told Your people who were up against a great enemy that the battle was not theirs but Yours. You said they wouldn't even need to fight; they could just stand and watch Your saving power at work. Please show me when I just need to stand still and stand strong and let You do all the fighting for me. Thank You! Amen.

DAY 192

Keep on Sinning? No!

Sin spread when the Law was given. But where sin spread, God's loving-favor spread all the more. Sin had power that ended in death. Now, God's loving-favor has power to make men right with Himself. It gives life that lasts forever. Our Lord Jesus Christ did this for us. What does this mean? Are we to keep on sinning so that God will give us more of His loving-favor? No, not at all! We are dead to sin. How then can we keep on living in sin?

Romans 5:20–6:2

Father God, Your grace and Your love are incredible. When sin spread, Your love spread. You want to take away the punishment of sin. You want to make all people right with You through Jesus and give them life that lasts forever. But no way should people ever think that sin doesn't matter. We should do our very best to keep away from sin because we are so grateful You have saved us from it. Amen.

DAY 193

You Belong to God

Do you not know that your body is a house of God where the Holy Spirit lives? God gave you His Holy Spirit. Now you belong to God. You do not belong to yourselves. God bought you with a great price. So honor God with your body. You belong to Him.

1 Corinthians 6:19–20

Lord God, because You saved me from my sin through Jesus' death on the cross, I believe that I am not my own—I belong to You! Your Holy Spirit lives in me, and I want to honor You with my body in everything I think and say and do. Show me the good things You want me to do and the bad things You want me to stay away from. Please help me to honor You well! Amen.

DAY 194

The God Who Made the World

"The God Who made the world and everything in it is the Lord of heaven and earth. He does not live in buildings made by hands. No one needs to care for Him as if He needed anything. He is the One who gives life and breath and everything to everyone. He made from one blood all nations who live on the earth. He set the times and places where they should live. They were to look for God. Then they might feel after Him and find Him because He is not far from each one of us. It is in Him that we live and move and keep on living."

ACTS 17:24–28

Dear Father God, thank You for being Lord of all! You give life and breath to every person and every creature. Everything comes from You! Thank You for caring so much about me and what I do. You've set the times and places for my life. I will keep looking to You all of my days. I'm so thankful You are always near. Amen.

DAY 195

Beautiful Feet

Everyone who calls on the name of the Lord will be saved from the punishment of sin. But how can they call on Him if they have not put their trust in Him? And how can they put their trust in Him if they have not heard of Him? And how can they hear of Him unless someone tells them? And how can someone tell them if he is not sent? The Holy Writings say, "The feet of those who bring the Good News are beautiful."

Romans 10:13–15

Dear Jesus, I don't really think much about my feet being nice looking or not. That's kind of funny! But please help me to have truly beautiful feet like Your Word talks about—feet that bring the good news about You and Your saving power to everyone around me who needs to hear it. Amen.

DAY 196

Much More

God is able to do much more than we ask or think through His power working in us. May we see His shining-greatness in the church. May all people in all time honor Christ Jesus. Let it be so.

EPHESIANS 3:20–21

Father God, I believe You can do so much more than anything I ask of You or imagine You can do! Whatever it is I'm hoping and praying for, You can go so far above and beyond. Help me to realize that if You don't answer my prayers the way I'm hoping for, it's because You have a bigger and better plan in mind. Help me to be content with however You choose to answer my prayers. You are almighty God, and I trust You in all things. Amen.

DAY 197

Joy and Peace, Not Worry

Be full of joy always because you belong to the Lord. Again I say, be full of joy! Let all people see how gentle you are. The Lord is coming again soon. Do not worry. Learn to pray about everything. Give thanks to God as you ask Him for what you need. The peace of God is much greater than the human mind can understand. This peace will keep your hearts and minds through Christ Jesus.

PHILIPPIANS 4:4–7

Dear Lord, I belong to You! Please fill me up with joy because of that truth. Help other people to see Your love and hope shining in me. I believe You are coming again soon at exactly the right time. Meanwhile, I don't need to worry. I just need to pray about everything, give thanks to You, and ask You for what I need. Then Your awesome peace will keep me and guide me. Thank You! Amen.

DAY 198

God Knows

"Are not five small birds sold for two small pieces of money? God does not forget even one of the birds. God knows how many hairs you have on your head. Do not be afraid. You are worth more than many small birds."

LUKE 12:6–7

Dear Father God, remind me how much You care about even tiny birds, so surely You care even more about me. It's mind-boggling to think that You even know the number of hairs on my head. That's incredible! No one else knows that! No one else would want to spend the time to count them. But You know every single little detail about me. I am so dearly loved by You, and that truth gives me confidence and courage. I don't need to be afraid of anything, because You are my Father. Amen.

DAY 199

The Lord Watches over You

The Lord watches over you. The Lord is your safe cover at your right hand. The sun will not hurt you during the day and the moon will not hurt you during the night. The Lord will keep you from all that is sinful. He will watch over your soul. The Lord will watch over your coming and going, now and forever.

Psalm 121:5–8

Dear Lord, thank You for watching over me every day and every night. You know everything I do and everywhere I go, and You are with me always, caring for me and keeping me safe. You watch over my soul now and forever. I love You and praise You! Amen.

DAY 200

Trusting in the Lord Forever

"You will keep the man in perfect peace whose mind is kept on You, because he trusts in You. Trust in the Lord forever. For the Lord God is a Rock that lasts forever."

ISAIAH 26:3–4

Lord, I believe this scripture is a promise for me—a promise that You will keep me in perfect peace when I keep my mind focused on You, focused on trusting in You. My mind likes to think about a lot of things, but the best is to think about You! I choose to trust in You every moment of every day forever! I believe You are the one true Lord God of all. You are a rock that lasts forever. I am so grateful I belong to You! Amen.